"I worked with in  saw the positive impa well as the damage do I met Londa through her ministry and could see God's love radiating through her but did not know the battles she faced each time she came to visit with the women incarcerated at my facility.

"In her book Londa illustrates the real struggle that will occur when bringing God's message. Satan is in a battle to claim as many souls as he can and will strew your path with numerous pitfalls in the hope you will give up. Londa encourages us to not fail and to GO. Each chapter brings encouragement even when it appears Satan has won. This book is a must read for any who are doing ministry work or are contemplating doing so."
Angela D. Ashley, Florida Department of Corrections (1982 -2005)
Bradenton Transitional Center (Director 2005-2011)

"Author Londa Duncan has offered us a spiritually valuable guide that is real usable, helpful, and practical. She starts with establishing facts and ends with making sure we can utilize them in all seasons of life and ministry. Ms. Duncan has faithfully ministered in women's prisons, substance abuse clinics, adoption centers, and churches. She has learned that 'the reality of our purpose is to recognize the enemies strategies and through God's power set the captives free.'

"I have known Londa for many years and have found her to be true in word and deed with a genuine determination to destroy the hold of Satan on lives and help those lives become new creations. Her title describes her mission: *GO! daily. The Gospel: Live it. Do it. Be it.* I recommend you read her book and GO do what it says!"
Dr. Terry Raburn, Superintendent,
Peninsular Florida District Council of the Assemblies of God,
Chairman of the Board of Trustees, Southeastern University

"No one will read this book and be the same person after the last page. The stories you are about to read, and the hope you will gain, will encourage you to GO daily and be the person God called and equipped you to be. Some of these stories I witnessed firsthand and others I have enjoyed reading. Open this book and be encouraged to be the light to someone that is in darkness as you GO Daily!"
Suzann Smith, Children's Minister

"When the apartment next to mine became vacant, I began to pray that the Lord would send just the right person to occupy it. How thankful I am that He chose Londa! Sometimes in the evenings after she had gotten home from ministry responsibilities, I would slip over to hear how the Lord had provided her with the wisdom needed to meet the interesting and unusual challenges of the day! I saw her concern for those she was counseling, shared her sorrow over those who were messing up, and rejoiced with her over those who had trusted Christ and who were beginning to grow. What a blessing and encouragement that was to me! Now, as we read these stories about what the Lord has done in Londa's life and in the lives of those with whom she works, let's pray we all may be challenged to GO daily and be what He wants us to be for His glory!"

Marilyn Phyllis Pitzer, retired Baptist Mid-Missions missionary

"I met Londa at a Kairos Prison ministry training over fifteen years ago. We volunteered weekly at the Hillsborough Correctional Institute for women for over seven years. We also worked together at a nine-month residential drug treatment center for women where I was the chaplain and Londa was a counselor.

"We have worked on the battlefield together outside the walls of the church. Londa is a great teacher who believes in the power of prayer and putting her faith into action. She is not afraid to teach truth and is very straightforward and direct.

"Londa has a heart of compassion for the downtrodden and those that everyone else has lost hope for, while believing that God can touch their lives."

Reverend Michele Mitchell, ED.D

"I was highly impressed with Londa's book *GO, Daily!* and it has changed my life! This is an incredibly thoughtful, unique, and special gift to help people improve their self-image, encourage them to have positive values and give back! I know that it will inspire many people not only to increase their self-confidence, but also determine the value and importance of obeying the Lord's commands! I can't wait to share this book with my friends!"

Samantha Smith, Adoptive Parent

"It is an honor for me to share about my friend Londa, who is a multi-talented woman of God. I remember the first time my husband, Hermel, and I saw her at a Sunday school class that caught our attention. The kids were worshiping the Lord in Spirit and in truth, they were praying and interceding with such intensity for the sick in the church that it touched our hearts and brought back memories of my childhood. We left there with a great impression of her.

"Later, as missionaries in Cape Town South Africa in 2004, we had invited a dear friend, Helen Campbell to come and teach leadership to pastors and ministers in Cape Town. She asked if she could bring a friend who was very good ministering to children. We asked for her friend's name and she said, Londa Duncan. Immediately we said yes. Londa shared the gospel with hundreds of children, and many of them gave their hearts to Jesus Christ.

"I can say of Londa that she is a woman who loves God and people. A lady of great integrity and compassion, when she embarks on any project or work, she does it with all her heart for the glory of God. She is not afraid to share the good news of Jesus Christ to anyone, anywhere, and anytime.

"I know this book and the stories in it will inspire and challenge you to GO as our Master has commanded us to reach that which is lost. You are about get blessed—so get ready!

Rev. Leslie Del Rosario, M.Rel.ed
Assemblies of God World Missionary

"A must-read treasure! Londa Duncan tells it like it is with real life heartfelt stories all pointing to how God uses us when we show up in service to Him. With a front row seat to her ministry journey, I can affirm that she is who she says she is. We've served together in prison ministry since 2005—showing up for the forgotten behind the razor wire. Be challenged and encouraged to GO Daily!"

Maggie Sabatier Smith, founder of Called To Action, Speaker, Coach

GO! DAILY

The Gospel: Live It. Do It. Be It.

Londa Duncan

RIVER BIRCH PRESS

Daphne, Alabama

River Birch Press
P.O. Box 868, Daphne, AL 36526

I offer thanks to my parents, Fred Duncan and Carolyn Ouellette,

who taught me to give and help others as a way of life each day.

Also, to my grandparents, Richard and Dorothy Cooprider,

who are now in the great cloud of witnesses in heaven.

Your footsteps I endeavor to step in

along life's journey.

Table of Contents

Preface

This book describes my journey and experiences over the years working in substance abuse, prison ministry, adoption, and ministry in many rough and ignored places. Woven through these experiences are lessons I learned, and the realization that the gospel of Jesus Christ is something we do and live. I have tried to share some of my stories and explain how they teach us to GO daily and fulfill the Great Commission.

I realized as I walked prison compounds, substance abuse centers, hospitals, and rough neighborhoods, that the gospel, and the freedom of the gospel, must be taken to the people. They are not coming to find it.

I stepped inside a substance abuse center in central Florida one day. My eyes became blurry as my foot crossed the threshold, and I immediately had a migraine headache. I am not prone to migraines. I checked in and walked to the modular to meet with women one-on-one. I told the woman I met with that she needed to pray for me. She said my condition resulted from witchcraft, as the women there were reading witchcraft books that someone had brought into the center. We took authority over the witchcraft, and the migraine left instantly.

Our purpose is to recognize the enemy's strategies and set the captives free through God's power.

To work in God's kingdom, we do not have to be a pastor or a well-known minister. We don't need a platform in the work of the gospel. The world is our platform, and our daily life is our journey. God positions us before those who need His light in dark places. And often, He does so on ordinary days.

I witnessed life given to a woman whose heart stopped twice in a Florida state prison when an unusual intersection of events occurred. She regained breath twice and lived. It was not because I had fasted and prayed or was more spiritual than anyone on the compound. I believe it was because I showed up and was present so God could give life through a willing vessel. God is God, and we should praise Him.

When we obey and GO, God will take us to places we never imagined we would GO. The Great Commission is for all days and seasons, not just on our good days and when we feel we are on spiritual heights. We GO even when we have made mistakes or when others disapprove.

We often GO through our pain and struggles, and God honors our obedience to bring light to an individual's darkness. I've gone tired and even aggravated, but God worked for the one to whom God sent me. I have learned that many people feel unnoticed in today's world, and a light bearer is needed to walk into their dark loneliness and shine a light to direct their way to freedom.

The hope within my heart is that the words and stories you are about to read will encourage you to go daily and be the person God created you to be. And may you go a little further than you ever have before!

1

Those Who Believed a Lie

I sat in my office in central Florida where I worked as a substance abuse counselor.

"I'm retarded, Ms. Londa."

"Who told you that?"

"I am."

"But who told you that?"

"Everyone. I've been told that I was retarded all my life."

"Did a professional diagnose you?"

"I don't know. But everyone has told me I'm retarded. I can't do my written assignments."

I could not get a clear answer as to why this young woman thought she was retarded other than people had told her that her entire life. Therefore, she believed she could not complete written assignments. I spoke with my clinical director, and we decided to ask her if she could draw her answers rather than write them. I reconstructed that portion of her treatment plan and then met with her.

"Do you think if I asked you a few questions, you could take a notebook and draw your answers rather than write them?"

"Sure. I'll give it a try."

I gave her the notebook and instructions. My next scheduled one-on-one with that client was eye-opening.

"Were you able to answer my questions with pictures?"
"Yes, ma'am."

She pulled her notebook out of a bag, opened it to her first drawing, and handed it to me. My mouth fell open. I was shocked. Beyond shocked! I expected stick figures; instead, I was looking at the work of an artist. A gifted artist. I looked up and said, "You're an artist. Your work is phenomenal. Your drawings are not something a person with cognitive delays could produce. You are not retarded. You have just been told a lie for so many years that you believed it. Do you care if I show the clinical director?"

She did not, and after the session, I was in my clinical director's office as soon as she was available.

"You have to see this!" She was as amazed as I was. "This girl is not retarded," I said. "She has just been lied to her entire life and believed it!"

Deceit

Deceit is the oldest trap of humankind, yet people step into its snare every day. God gave us a brain, but that doesn't seem to stop us at times. Deceit is the tool Satan used to cause the fall of humanity in the garden of Eden. Genesis 3 tells the story. Satan asked a question and made a statement; consequently, the fall of humankind occurred, and we are dealing with the results to this day. It would seem that this fall into sin would have been more dramatic, but it was predicated on deceit. It worked. It accomplished the purpose of the enemy of our souls. The man and woman believed the lie and risked everything by reasoning with a lie.

The question: "Has God indeed said, 'You shall not eat of every tree of the garden?'" (Genesis 3:1) And when the woman tried to explain and reason with deceit, Satan replied with a misleading statement: "You will not surely die!" (Genesis 3:4). That was all it took to transform sinless humanity into fallen creatures in need of redemption.

Why didn't Satan rush into the garden with all the forces of hell and, by fear and intimidation, force the man and woman to sin and follow his agenda? Perhaps that would be too obvious. Instead, he reasoned through deception until Adam and Eve believed the lie.

In John 8:44, Jesus described Satan when speaking with a group of Jews who did not believe in Him and whose reasoning made little sense:

> *You are of your father the devil, and the desires of your father you want to do. He was a murderer from the beginning, and does not stand in the truth, because there is no truth in him. When he speaks a lie, he speaks from his own resources [opinions], for he is a liar and the father of it.*

The father of lies is no respecter of persons. After working as a substance abuse counselor, I was employed in an adoption agency in Florida, working with birth mothers to place their babies for adoption. During my job there, I once asked a young pregnant woman who was riding in the car with me, "Have you ever worked?"

"No, I can't," she said.

"Why not?"

"I stutter."

I glanced over at her. "People who stutter can work as easily as people who do not stutter."

"I, I, uh, I can't, Ms. Londa."

"Did you graduate high school?

"No, ma'am."

3

"How far did you go in school?"

"The ninth grade and spent t-time with my boyfriend until we got m-married."

"You can get a GED. I'd be glad to help you."

"I can't."

"Because of the drugs?"

"Yes!"

I looked at her again. "You know, people who want help get help. There are many people in this world who have come out of addictions. Many people as adults get a high school diploma. And they are all just people. If they did it, so can you."

But she believed a lie. She believed she could not.

One of the last times I was with that young lady occurred one evening. It was 5:30 p.m. and time for me to go home for the day. My boss received a call. Some jerk had dumped the woman out on the side of the road in another town, and she needed help. Our agency was responsible for ensuring the unborn baby and the mother were safe.

Why can't these people have emergencies during regular business hours? I thought. I had been up since five that morning, and I admit I was tired and complaining to myself. That young pregnant girl was high on meth and could not tell me her exact location. I drove to the town where she stated she was stranded while speaking to her on the cell phone.

"What street are you on?"

"I don't know."

"Do you see a street sign?"

"No, but I'm on the main road going into town."

"Can you give me a landmark?"

"What's that?"

"Is there a restaurant or store near you?"

"I don't know, but I'm by the carwash." Three car washes were located on that six-lane road. To make matters worse, it was getting dark when I finally spotted her. I was heading eastbound, and she was in the right lane of the westbound traffic. Dancing. Yes, dancing on the highway!

Oh great! I thought. "Lord, please don't let anyone hit her." I had to drive until I could find a lane to make a U-turn and get back to her. I lowered the window and instructed her to get out of the road. Thank God she did. As I pulled into the car wash parking lot, she opened the passenger door before I stopped the car. To avoid injuring her, I quickly stopped. I heard a loud siren and saw police lights behind me as a deputy in a patrol car motioned for me to pull forward.

"Whatever you have done, you better tell me now!"

"I didn't d-do anything, M-Ms. Londa."

The officer just wanted me to pull forward so he could proceed and wash his car, so I took a deep breath and moved forward! I drove back to the office where my boss and I stayed with the girl for several hours until she felt better.

"I'll take you home now."

"No, I don't want to be alone tonight."

"Where do you want to go?"

She wanted to go to a town about eight miles away to a trap house where she spent many nights. A trap house is a home owned or rented by a drug dealer who runs an illegal business in that location. We drove for a while, and then she decided she did not want to go there. She told me to take her to meet a man, and since I knew him, I agreed to meet him at a liquor store parking lot near his home. He supplied a lot of her drugs but would not harm her in any other way. On the drive to the liquor store, we had our final conversation.

"Ms. Londa, the voices are getting worse. Am I crazy? Is it demons? What is going on?"

I explained all the possibilities and the root causes of voices and night terrors in addicts, as well as scriptural reasons.

"But am I going to hell?"

That question opened a long and serious conversation where I could tell this young woman the truth—not what she heard in church growing up, not what people repeat as truth because it is what everyone says, but what God's Word says. I explained that God's love for her cannot be stopped because of her sins or her meth addiction.

I explained the Bible is not just a book. It is full of words from God's mouth to our eyes and ears. It is for all time. And it is for her. And salvation is not just going to a church or listening to a sermon. Salvation is a personal relationship with God. She also asked how to deal with evil spirits that were tormenting her. I have found it interesting that the world often recognizes evil spirits and their torment more than the children of the light do. I told her to read specific scriptures out loud and tell those tormentors to leave her alone.

We had a good talk while driving. The time of that drive allowed me to speak truth to her. I did not realize it until later, but I think the pregnant woman was sober in the car that night. It was one of the few times I had seen her sober in several years of knowing her. I believe God sobered her to give her those moments in that car with a woman who was tired, aggravated, and wanted to go home, yet spoke the truth to her.

God doesn't use us because we are super spiritual. He uses us because we show up. The prophet Samuel explained in 1 Samuel 15:22: "To obey is better than sacrifice."

God works through the voice, the hands, and the feet of

those who desire to please Him. Our mandate is to go, and our method is obedience.

I attended that young mother's funeral a short time later. Accidental overdose. If someone had told that young woman years ago that she had believed a lie and that she could graduate school and work and be successful, would my car sermon not have been needed? I can only hope so.

Addicts, criminals, and the hard-hearted can be more exhausting work than anyone can imagine who has never ventured into that harvest field. And yet, Jesus said, "Go."

Sometimes taking the light to darkness doesn't look how we think it should.

Believing a lie is just what the enemy wants for humanity. Deceit robs us of the freedom God provided by taking our minds captive to a lie. Once a person believes a lie, they speak it, act on it, and reap its consequences. James 1:14–15 says,

> But each one is tempted when he is drawn away by his own desires and enticed. Then, when desire has conceived, it gives birth to sin; and sin, when it is full-grown, brings forth death.

The lie is conceived, gives birth to sin, matures, and results in spiritual and often physical death. God designed us to enjoy freedom in our lives, and Jesus died on the cross to give us that freedom. The tool that deprives us of freedom is deceit. Satan hates our God-given liberty and uses every weapon at his disposal to convince us we are not free in Christ.

When living in God's truth and freedom, we live our lives differently than before being set free. Our worship becomes the work of our hands every day. Our lives take on purpose as we see we have a mandate for each new day. We prosper in our spiritual walk, mentality, accomplishments, and finances. The lies that fly into our lives on the back of fiery darts come with the intent to destroy the liberation God provided for His children. For this purpose, Jesus came and provided freedom. For this same purpose, we go and destroy the deceit and lies.

I've seen lies fully grown in many people's lives. A young man and woman were so mature in their deceit that they threw all caution to the wind with their lives and their unborn baby's life.

The man said to me, "I know what you think of me and what you're gonna say. You're gonna tell me I'm a big man because I beat on women. I've heard it too many times. You're too late!"

"No," I replied, "I don't think you're a big man. I think you're a jerk and an idiot! And if you ever harm this young woman and that baby she is carrying, I have no problem calling the law! So again, you are not a big man! And if you think I'm afraid of you, you are wrong! I have met much bigger bears in prison and elsewhere than your skinny little butt. In my presence you will treat this young lady with respect, and you will treat me with respect. Try me if you don't believe me. I will stop this vehicle and put your sorry butt on the side of the road. I will leave you standing there, and "big man" can get himself home! And furthermore, it's "Yes, ma'am," and "No ma'am," for you!"

Meet baby daddy. Also known as one that lives off yours and my tax dollars. This man gets food stamps and Medicaid and lives with baby mama during each pregnancy. He supplements the support she gets for housing, utilities, food, phone, etc., by selling drugs and committing crimes. And he usually has more than one baby mama, so he is a "big man."

He asked me, "If I get arrested, are you gonna come and get me out of jail?"

"No, but if she gets arrested, I will come and see her."

"You mean if I go to jail, you won't come and see me, Ms. Londa?"

"No."

After the second or third horrific and brutal beating this young girl endured from "big man," and after we realized it was a miracle she had not miscarried or died, I looked at her and said, "He is going to kill you one of these days."

"Well, ya gotta go some way."

"But you don't gotta go that way!"

She believed a lie!

The meth was too powerful, and "big man" was her connection. She believed a lie that she could not live without him or meth.

Take a moment and look at the Bible through this lens: Satan is a liar and a murderer, and he has no truth. God Almighty is truth and has no deceit or sin in Him. Satan's entire agenda and warfare strategies are based on deception, his weapon of war. He doesn't care which lie someone believes. Just believe one, reject the truth, and destroy your life. Pick a lie, any lie. Just pick one:

- I am retarded.
- I cannot work.
- You gotta go some way.

And a few more:
- God is love, so I can live and love any way I choose.
- I am a woman trapped in a man's body.
- It is my choice and my body, and I can choose abortion.

And on and on and on.

Just take one. Believe one. It doesn't matter what the lie might be, just so the weapon of deceit succeeds. And when the individual eats the fruit and sin enters, the deception destroys that person's life gradually and daily.

The alternative is God's way—the truth. We can choose to believe it or not. We can reject the selfish "me-first" and "what I want I want" mentality and opt for the truth. The gospel message is simple. Believe the truth and act on it, or believe a lie and act on it. But we must choose one. And many people will remain in deceit and never hear the truth if you and I do not GO and tell them.

When we GO daily, we endeavor to unlock the chains of deceit that hold individuals in a prison of darkness. We must shine light into the darkness of deception. Snakes, rats, and roaches hide in darkness. Destruction hides in the darkness of deceit until one steps in with the light and reveals the truth that sets a person free.

2

The Unnoticed

The Bible clarifies how our faith should appear to others in James 2:15–17:

If a brother or sister is naked and destitute of daily food, and one of you says to them, depart in peace, be warmed and filled, but you do not give them the things which are needed for the body, what does it profit? Thus also faith by itself, if it does not have works, is dead.

When asked in Matthew 22:36–39 which commandment is the greatest, Jesus said,'

You shall love the Lord your God with all your heart. This is the first and great commandment. And the second is like it: You shall love your neighbor as yourself."

Over the years, I have heard many believers say God didn't call them to the prisons or to those types of people. Many people think you must be a special person to work with prisoners. Yes, you do. It is called an obedient person. Obedient to the mandate of our Lord to GO to them. We GO and He equips us.

Many people in this world feel unseen. In 2005, I began serving on a Kairos Prison Ministry team. This group goes into a prison for a four-day retreat to teach inmates the love of God and the basics of salvation. Their follow-up program is superb. Teams of women GO into women's prisons, and teams of men GO into men's prisons. Two team members and one clergy sit at each table throughout the weekend with the same group of inmates.

One weekend, a woman who sat to my right was from Daytona Beach, Florida. After hearing the teachings on Thursday night (the first night), she began to cry and ask, "Why didn't someone ever tell me this? Why didn't I ever hear this? I wouldn't be here had I known!"

I continued working with that woman throughout that weekend and until closing on Sunday afternoon. Being curious, I quizzed her.

"Did you ever go to Sunday school?"

"Did any Christians ever knock on your door?"

"Did anyone ever offer to take you to a church or pick you up on a bus?"

"Did you ever see a preacher on TV or hear one on the radio?"

"Did anyone ever try to talk to you about Jesus or having a relationship with Him?"

Her answer to every question was no.

I was stunned. I had just met a person who had never heard the gospel message one time in America! A woman raised in Daytona Beach, Florida. How did this happen in such a bustling location? Why didn't someone somewhere at some time GO to her? That woman felt she had been unnoticed by those who could have helped her before her incarceration.

I have never met a prostitute who showed up at church on

a Sunday morning. Never met a gang member or addict that strolled into church for a service. Someone must GO to them. That "someone" is you and me. We are the church, and it is our responsibility to go.

Kairos asked throughout the weekend, "Who is the church?" And we all answered, "We are the church!" Which is the point I am trying to make. We are the church who our Lord mandates to go!

I have spent a reasonable amount of time in my work in the hood and among people who think no one beyond their neighborhood sees them. Poverty and being unnoticed makes one a slave to misery. Take a ride with me into the Section 8 housing units. Make sure your car door is locked as we approach.

As we turn into the parking lot of the massive two-story apartment buildings spread out for blocks, we notice the trash scattered everywhere. Yes, everywhere! A dumpster is at the end of each pod, but why use that? Set your trash bags anywhere in the parking lot or on the grass. Throw bottles, soda cans, cups, straws, drug paraphernalia, dirty diapers, paper towels, styrofoam containers from the local restaurant, grocery bags, candy wrappers, chicken bones, cigars, and cigarettes. By now, you should get the picture. Trash and garbage are everywhere! Don't let the toddler pick up a used needle. Wait, where is the adult supposed to be watching that little one?

Young men in their teens, twenties, and thirties are standing on the corner during work hours. Several have guns in their pockets, waistbands, or hands and are selling drugs. I have always enjoyed driving into these areas. Residents thought I was either the Department of Children and Families, a caseworker, a detective, or some agency from which they wanted to run. I have cleared parking lots by simply driving in.

While working in adoption, I drove into the parking lot of a Section 8 apartment complex. Some teenagers stood in front of my vehicle and acted like they did not see me, so I could not leave. No problem. I had a conversation with the birth mother who lived there. She explained to the teenagers that I was her mother (her white mother) and described what she would do if they ever bothered me again. After that, I received the utmost respect when driving in that neighborhood.

Wasp nests hang on every building, bush, and window. Why should the complex bother to kill them? Why do they care? No one else does. Don't forget about the rats, roaches, and filth. After going into some birth mothers' apartments, when I got home, I took my shoes off outside and put my clothes in a plastic garbage bag until I could wash them. Not all live that way, but many do.

Most people in this lifestyle have no chance of ever coming out of their hopeless cycle. They hope for a brighter future, but it has not arrived. No one has noticed them. Poverty is slavery, and God calls us to GO to people ensnared in its trap and show them a better way.

These are often the places we want to avoid visiting. Doing so is not glamorous, and we receive no applause. But we GO because our Lord instructed us to GO. Ministry is not always on a platform. It is snatching people from the fire and rescuing those in danger. Ministry is turning the light on in their darkness so they may see the way out of hopelessness. They need to be seen by someone who can help them. True love notices them.

In the adoption field, I often have been called to homes where the baby daddy abused mothers and fights were occurring. I've been to homes where the police came and called the

Department of Children and Families (DCF) or where DCF came to remove the children. Often landlords would call me rather than call the police because they did not want their community to receive a bad rating and reputation. I would tell them repeatedly to call the police, but they would call me. I have ordered abusive young men off the premises of property the agency owned or rented. I told them if they abused the mother or the children, I had no problem calling the Sheriff's Department. And I did.

Situations like these are where the lack of light in the darkness and having no direction in life leads. God created people to have a purpose. Why else would we exist? Idle hands and unchallenged minds lead to trouble. Lack of intentions leads to destruction. But who notices them?

I received a call years ago to GO to the home of a young woman I had tried to help for some time. A relative had tried to kill one of the children in the family. Someone walked in on the scene and averted the tragedy. The child lived, but one cannot forget situations like that. When Jesus gave us His command to GO into all the world, He meant *all* the world.

Ministry is messy and hard. Full of mistakes, failures, pain, and frustration, reality is complicated. A sinful world is full of sin, and a dark world is full of darkness. We must be light in the darkness. Most of the time, shining brightly in a dark world is not easy, nor is it fair. But life is not fair. We must work hard to accomplish our purpose on this earth.

People often stay in bondage because they do not know the way out, but they also think no one who can help sees them. They are hidden in their darkness and from the children of the light.

One day I was taking a birth mother, a hard-core meth addict, home from an appointment. Well, not home, but to one of the trap houses where she sometimes stayed in town. She was high, irritable, paranoid, and acting out. I was a few blocks from the house where she asked me to take her. As she became increasingly agitated, she opened the car door and jumped out. Thank God I was going very slowly as I had just turned a corner. She was very pregnant but not harmed. Again, these are the actions of someone with no purpose who has believed a lie about herself and life in general. She felt unnoticed and drowned herself in meth.

The adoption agency had to force a mother and her baby daddy to leave our one-bedroom trailer owned by the agency. This was after she lost her baby, and they refused to move within the fair amount of time we gave them. We gave them time to find a place, treated them well, and they finally left.

After the couple vacated the property, I assessed the damage, which was in the top three worst of all I had seen. When they would fight, the baby daddy would punch or kick the wall, and every wall in that trailer had multiple holes ranging from a few inches to several feet. The bathroom door was torn off the hinges. The cabinet doors were damaged and hanging. Windows were broken, the back door was damaged, and much more.

They had broken out the front windows more than once while fighting. The place was so trashed that my boss was unsure if she should remodel it or have it torn down. Why did we not GO after them for damages? How do you get money from people who do not work and move around from couch to couch? You do not. They simply do not care.

That young man and woman needed to be noticed at a

young age and disciplined with secure boundaries. Often our part is teaching practical lessons in life, such as morals, anger management, responsibility, manners, and how to live as decent human beings. God can save and change anyone, but they need to be taught many lessons, which is our responsibility. I have met hundreds of young women whose parents never noticed they needed to be taught how to live life.

People are stuck in their slavery of poverty, no purpose, and destructive lifestyles. I believe if Jesus were on earth today, He would be out among those in darkness. The darkness covers them, and they are not seen. Therefore, they go deeper into destruction. Jesus would shine a light for the addict and the abused woman, the abused child, and the young man on the street corner selling drugs with no purpose in life.

Someone needs to show up with light and answers. If you don't know where to start, feed someone hungry. Befriend someone lonely. Talk to the person behind you in the grocery line, post office, or restaurant. People are often overlooked, and they appreciate and feel valued when someone talks to them.

Let me give you an example. I lived in Lakeland, Florida, and was in Bartow, Florida, often for my work. I began noticing a young man on the streets in Bartow who was very thin and in poor condition. His beard looked as if he had not touched it in several years and was long and matted. His hair was matted, and his clothes were worn. I saw him repeatedly in Bartow for months. As I drove by, I would think, *How sad a situation.*

One day, I noticed the man in a drug store parking lot not far from my home in Lakeland. I wondered how long it took him to make that journey on foot from Bartow. He looked to be thinner and in worse shape.

A friend came by my house one day and stated she had seen the man camping at the edge of a lake full of alligators near my home. She was very concerned about his welfare if he attempted to bathe in the lake. Often homeless people in Florida bathe in lakes, and gators have attacked or killed many of them. We were concerned but not sure what to do. I had seen the man in the drug store parking lot pointing at something I could not see and screaming. I did not know if he was on drugs or mentally ill. *And was he safe to approach?*

The months dragged on, and the man seemed to be staying in the antique district of the town. I noticed one day as I passed him in my car that his pants were now threadbare. He had worn them so long that the material was shredding away, and his skin was exposed to the elements. God began to deal with my heart that action needed to be taken for this man. *But what could I do?*

On a drive not long after that day, I noticed him sitting in an alcove of a large downtown building, shading himself from the sun and facing a busy road. He was staring at nothing in particular. I watched cars go by, and it was as if he were invisible. There was a human whose pants consisted of a waistband, pockets, and shreds of material, and people drove by and did not even notice him. God gave me a revelation as I looked at him in that alcove. The man was so unseen and far from human interaction that he no longer wanted to be seen.

God made clear to me that this man was unnoticed by the city but not by God. Becoming invisible to humans, overlooked or looked through, was his existence. People did not even look his way. *How must he feel? What was this doing to his mind?* I wondered how it must feel for a young man to walk down a busy street with his hair matted, his beard mangled and long, with pants that looked like someone had cut them into strips of material. He had no self-worth or respect. He had to be humiliated.

I heard God's still, small voice instructing me to buy him clothes and food. I continued to drive out of my way to ensure I knew where he slept and spent his days. Of course, he did not know that; I was just another car going by. I bagged the clothes, underwear, toiletries, and food and left my driveway one day, hoping to connect with him. I found him sitting beside a doctor's office on the sidewalk. I pulled up to the red light, rolled down the window, and said, "Hey, buddy, this is for you." The man stood up, walked to the car door, and gently took the bags from me. I told him to have a good day and drove off.

I was curious to know if he used the items. I continued to drive through town in hopes I could see him. He ate the food but carried the clothes in a bag. I wondered if they did not fit or if he didn't understand.

Then one Saturday morning, I was en route to plans for my day off. I stopped at the same red light, and there he was. "Give him money," I heard in my spirit. The light turned green, and I had to go as traffic was behind me. I heard it again. "Give him money." I knew it wouldn't stop, so I drove a huge circle to get to a side street and drove up to the light by the corner where he sat. No one was behind me now. I rolled down the window and held out a folded twenty-dollar bill. "Hey, buddy. This is for you."

The man stood up and walked to the car window. I handed him the bill. He looked down at it and said, "Well, thank you."

He spoke! Human contact and compassion broke through to him. I told him to have a good day and drove on. A few weeks later, I saw the man walking down a sidewalk in the town near the mission. He had on the clothes I bought him, his beard was short and neatly trimmed, and his hair was cut and styled. He even walked with his head up.

Then it dawned on me! Most missions require a small fee for a night's stay. The twenty dollars got him into the mission, and they started his care. He just needed one person to notice that he was a human being. Under that matted beard and shredded pants was a person that had lost all dignity and human recognition.

How do we GO daily? Just start looking around when you drive down a street. Watch those in your neighborhood and your workplace. We can extend a hand to someone daily to lead them out of darkness and pain. Sometimes they just need to be noticed.

3

Planned Parenthood

If you had told me years ago I would be speaking at a local Planned Parenthood training, I would have probably thought you were insane. But it happened. God doesn't use us because we are so spiritual and wonderful. God uses us because we show up and obey. And therein lies the problem for many. They do not show up anywhere except the church building.

At the time of my Planned Parenthood encounter, I was not the executive director of the adoption agency but the liaison for biological mothers who entered adoption plans. My boss and the executive director asked me to attend a meeting with them. Our executive director had a connection with Planned Parenthood. They were conducting training on a certain day and had asked if she would teach a session on adoption, as they wanted to offer adoption to their clients. I was skeptical.

Our executive director agreed to conduct the training but had to go out of town during that time. The responsibility fell to me. God has a way of getting His people where He wants them to GO and do what He wants them to do.

I was to present adoption, the process, and a woman's choice in adoption. "Just prepare your teaching and let me review it, and we will discuss it then," my boss told me. I had spoken publicly, but never at a venue like Planned Parenthood. My boss and the executive director asked, "Are you nervous?"

"No! They will love me. You will be proud." I went home that night and prayed!

I prepared my notes and later submitted them to my boss, who approved them. My job was to find a way to present adoption to an abortion clinic and do it so that they would listen to me and not turn a deaf ear immediately. I have hated abortion from the first time I understood what it was as a young girl. I had no intention or reason ever to set foot into an abortion clinic, and now I was scheduled to train an entire abortion clinic on adoption.

The day of the training came. I was to arrive at lunchtime for my session. I pulled into the parking lot, gathered my belongings, and entered the building. I asked for the director of training who had scheduled my workshop, who greeted me with enthusiasm.

We learned we had attended the same high school and knew many of the same people. The director called the employees to the lobby where we held the training. They trickled in one by one. Some were polite, some did not speak, and a few people avoided looking my way. I am not insecure, and that did not bother me. I guess if I were in their shoes, I might be skeptical too. I could tell they were in attendance because they were required to do so, not because they chose to be there.

I was given a time limit for my session and agreed to comply. I am not the kind of person who thinks I have the right to take other people's time. If I have a time limit, I stay within that boundary.

All the employees were women, and most were young women. The room was rectangular, with chairs lining the edges.

I sat at one end. The employees sat on the two sides. One older woman came and sat in the first chair on the left side of the room, and her demeanor told me she viewed me as the enemy.

Eventually, the doctor entered the room. I learned how to read body language from college classes, and we used it daily in the drug rehabilitation program. I notice it regularly. The doctor wore her white coat and sat on the right side of the room, about three chairs down from me. She crossed her legs and intertwined them, crossed her arms tightly against her abdomen, and turned sideways in her chair, facing away from me. She was not comfortable with the situation or with me.

I introduced myself and began my training. I had been told that Planned Parenthood majors on a women's right to choose and that I must stress that in adoption the mother's right and choice are paramount, which is the truth. It was beyond quiet in the room when the older woman to my left spoke up and asked about a birth mother's choice.

I explained how girls come to the adoption agency, how we do not coerce, and what the Florida statutes mandate. I laid out the mother's choice of adoption, even up to the point of signing the consent in the hospital. The woman said she had heard women do not get a choice at the hospital and are pressured to sign the consent for adoption. She was not being kind or respectful, so I took that as a challenge and expounded on the subject until even a child could understand.

At that point, a young woman sitting about two seats down from the older woman looked at me and said, "Can I say something?"

"Of course," I replied.

Everyone turned and looked at her, and I braced myself for the next line of fire.

She said, "No one in this room knows about this except our director, but I placed a child for adoption."

Whoa! What is God doing here? I thought.

The other women in the room began saying to her, "We didn't know that. Why didn't you ever tell us?"

The young woman replied that she honestly did not think they would understand.

She then pointed at me and said with great emphasis, "Everything this woman is saying is the truth! Everything! When I placed my baby for adoption, the attorney started to read the consent to me at the hospital, and I started crying. The attorney stopped, came over to me, and asked if I needed more time. She said she could come back the next day. No one coerced me. No one withheld my rights." She pointed at me again and said, "This woman is telling us the truth!"

I didn't know what to say except, "Thank you." Brilliant, I know. I looked at the clock, and my time was about over. I told the director we would have to end the session as my time was up, and it was about time for her training session to begin. She looked at me and said, "No, no, continue, please."

So, I did. I taught, the women listened, and I answered questions. I then told the director we needed to close as we were now into her session time.

"No," she said, "this is going well. Continue." So, I did. It is hard to describe the wonder of defending and explaining life in a baby slaughtering center. After a little while, I looked at the director once again and said, "Your session time is about over. I will stop now." She replied, "No, just take the rest of my time. I can do my session later." So, I did.

After I completed the workshop, I thanked the ladies for allowing me to come. They went back to their workstations, but several thanked me for coming and said they enjoyed our time together. I went to the doctor before she had a chance to stand up, reached out my hand, and told her I was glad I could meet her. She shook my hand and quickly disappeared through the door that led to the exam rooms.

The training director asked if I had brought brochures that I could leave for any clients who asked about adoption. I told her I would bring some by the next day. I kept my word. The ladies were excited to see me when I entered the lobby the next day with a box full of brochures, plastic stands, and business cards. They instructed me to come through the door and into the back hallway. They took the box and talked for a few minutes.

As I faced the desk, patient rooms were behind me. I was about to leave when a door opened, and the doctor walked out into the hallway. She came up to me, gave me a big bear hug so tight I thought she would break a rib, and then looked directly into my eyes. Her face expressed extreme pain. I put my hand on her arm and looked into her empty eyes. I said, "I'm glad I got to see you today." She shook her head up and down in a yes motion, never spoke a word, and darted into the next patient's room. I saw torment and emptiness on her face, and I read the look of darkness.

I left a business card with the training director and told the ladies goodbye. As I exited through the lobby, a young couple sat waiting to be called for their appointment. A couple of other young women waited in the lobby as well. I glanced at each of them and wondered about their intent. I put my hand on the door, pushed it open, and went to my car. I sat and prayed for the young people in the lobby, the doctor, and all the employees.

I never heard from any of them again. I don't know what became of my words that day or what seeds have been watered by others. I know that I am just a human who showed up and obeyed. I also know what I learned from that experience.

The women I met in that clinic had believed many lies. From the older woman's questions to the young woman who had placed a child for adoption, to the doctor who lived in anguish, there were many pages of stories in their lives. And somewhere in those stories, they had believed a lie that led to where they were that day when a woman from an adoption agency showed up to teach a workshop at Planned Parenthood.

That day, my job was to walk into one of the darkest places and be a light. I had to stay focused in my workshop and not think of what had occurred behind those exam doors. I was fully aware that the light in me shone brightly in the darkness. I am confident that on a lunch hour in the lobby of a Planned Parenthood, the light shone so brightly that they have to remember it even if they do not understand.

The doctor was fighting an internal struggle, and it was apparent externally. Maybe she needed to be noticed, and the light turned on in her tormenting blackness. That look and that bear hug. I am still unclear about their meaning, but I do know by the Spirit of God, she saw the light that day. I prayed that God's convicting power would engulf her.

God is not limited to our way of doing things. Until we expand the view of our purpose in this life and how things have always been done, we will remain in our routine. I have been to many places where I never dreamed I would be. Not because I had fasted and prayed or am more spiritual than the next person. It was definitely not because I had not sinned. I believe it is simply because I showed up. God needs us to be there, and when we are, God works miracles and fulfills His purpose.

One of the greatest parts of this story is that not many people knew I went to Planned Parenthood and shared with them about adoption and life until now. I think the greatest acts we do for God are on ordinary days, often difficult ones, when we show up and obey. He does the rest.

We must look at abortion for what it is: the slaughter of the most vulnerable among us, the unborn. Through the years in prison ministry, drug rehabs, and the adoption field, I have spoken more times than I can count with women suffering the consequences of past abortions.

I want to offer hope and God's love to any woman who has ended her baby's life in abortion. The first step is to be honest with yourself and with God. Abortion is murder. If you are living with the guilt of abortion, you must begin by admitting that sin to God.

I have seen what abortion does to women. Over the years, it eats at your conscience. Guilt and regret begin to chip at your soul. You wonder how that child would have looked. *What about their personality? Would they have had your hair or eye color?*

Maybe you have made excuses that your aborted baby is better off since you could not afford to care for them. You could not offer opportunities they would need. Or maybe your addictions would have destroyed their life.

The time is now to realize excuses never provide a reason to end a life. As much as it may hurt, if you will admit the entirety of the truth to yourself and to God, He will provide forgiveness and healing. If you do not, the aftereffects of abortion will destroy you.

I have seen the effects of abortion crop up years later in the following ways:

- Guilt
- Low self-esteem
- Drugs
- Alcohol
- Difficulty in relationships
- Overcompensating
- Domestic violence
- Divorce
- Mental health issues
- Anger
- Eating disorders
- Criminal behavior
- Depression
- Health problems
- Anxiety
- Self-hatred
- Cutting

And I have also observed many other problems not listed. Often women could not find the root of their problems until confessing, repenting, forgiving themselves, and being forgiven of abortion.

I have met women who have had six or more abortions, and each one destroyed a part of their soul. Each abortion caused more destruction in their life. I have also met women who have told me they have no regrets and would do it again. My response is to ask if they think their life in prison, their addiction, their mental health problems and more are what they consider to be living a life of no regrets.

The guilt from abortion can sometimes eat away at a woman's health and peace of mind without them even realizing it. This guilt is similar to grief, with frequent days of frustration, weakness, depression, or regret. The person does not know these feelings are due to their grief.

A friend of mine realized this after the death of her mother. About a year had passed since her mother's death, and she was in a bad mood and frustrated. She walked through her house, and after glancing at the calendar, realized her mother's birthday was approaching. She then understood the grief was gnawing at her even when she did not realize it. That is how unforgiven sin destroys its victim, and that is how an unforgiven abortion could destroy a mom in that situation.

Often we believe the lie that our sin is worse than another's, and we cannot be free. Do not believe that lie. All sin is sin. And your sin can be forgiven. I encourage any woman who has had an abortion to allow God to forgive you. Your babies are in heaven and are waiting for you to join them one day. You may have taken life from them on this earth, but do not deny them the opportunity to spend eternity with you in heaven.

Jesus said in Matthew 19:14:

Suffer the little children [permit and let them], and forbid them not [do not hinder or prevent them], to come unto me, for of such [this] is the kingdom of heaven (Blue Letter Bible, 2022), [author's explanation].

All babies who died in abortion are in heaven. Jesus said for of such as these, little children, is the kingdom of heaven. You cannot go back and change the past. You cannot change the fact that you ended the life of your baby. But you can repent and spend eternity in heaven with them. I personally think when you enter heaven, Jesus will reunite you with that precious child. I also believe aborted babies get special attention from the Lord and others in heaven.

King David and Bathsheba conceived a child in sin and the baby died. After the death of the child, David explained why he stopped fasting and praying for the child in 2 Samuel 12:23: "I shall go to him, but he shall not return to me."

King David knew the child was safe with God and could not return to him on earth. He determined that he would go to the child once he died.

When you repent, your healing will begin. Forgive yourself. Yes, you can do it. Forgiveness is not a feeling—it is a choice. When you do forgive, you will begin to notice a difference in your health, your emotions, and your well-being. You cannot carry the burden of murder and shame. Jesus died on the cross and was punished for your abortions. He took that punishment and shame so that you do not have to carry it any longer.

Reach out to God and to someone who can help you. Freedom and forgiveness are for everyone.

4

Dispel the Lies

I sat at a picnic table shaded by an oak tree to lessen the intensity of the Florida sunshine. I was meeting with women one-on-one at a rehab/transitional center on the west coast of Florida. Women completed their last eighteen months or so of their prison term and received substance abuse therapy, employment, and many life skills and practical classes.

"Ms. Londa, I'm gay."

"Why do you think that?" I asked.

"Because I was a tomboy when I was a little girl."

"So was I." She looked at me as if I had interrupted her prepared speech. "How does being a tomboy as a little girl make you gay as a grown woman?"

"Well, I don't know, except . . . well, I just am."

As the conversation continued, I said, "You are not giving me answers. You are making excuses. And you are telling me you cannot serve God because your lifestyle does not agree with His Word. Yet you cannot give me a clear answer about how being a tomboy as a child made you gay. If you are going to base your life and eternity on something, you should, at the bare minimum, be able to intelligently explain and defend it.

"I think little girls go through tomboy stages to keep them from maturing too fast. We need a childhood. Girls mature faster than boys, and I believe it is God's protection in our childhood. I climbed trees, jumped off the garage roof into piles of leaves, and beat up neighborhood boys, to name a few of my childhood accomplishments. The only difference between you and me is that you believed a lie and I did not."

God is not confused, but many people today are. The Creator knows what He created and made no mistakes. If we believe He is confused, we have no hope. The force/being that spoke this universe into existence was accurate in His creation to design the human brain and all bodily systems, create birds to fly, cows to produce milk, fish to swim, and trees to provide shade. He proves His power by the alphabet written on each person's DNA. How can this God be confused about a human's gender or sexuality? He is not!

People believe lies, and this young woman believed a lie.

Homosexual. Gay. Lesbian. Transgender. Pedophiles. Modern culture wants us to believe these are alternative lifestyles. When did human beings have the right in God's creation to create an alternative lifestyle? Let's start with this lie. If you stick with this chapter to the end, you may realize God knew what He was doing. Left to our own imaginations, human beings can pervert anything.

Over the years, I have heard many people offer defenses for homosexual lifestyles. Ecclesiastes 1:9 says, "And there is nothing new under the sun." People have been falling for the same lies of Satan since the fall of man. Each generation thinks they have conceived something that no one had ever imagined before. Not so. There is nothing new under the sun. In all the places my life's journey has taken me, I have learned that people give the same excuses no matter their current situation.

Here are some general excuses for those in these lifestyles:

- I was born this way.
- I have always been attracted to the same sex.
- I don't believe the Bible is true.
- The Bible contains metaphors and sound principles, but it is not literal.
- God is love and wants us to love in any way we desire.
- How could a God of love condemn me for loving?

These are only some of the so-called reasons, but they are an excellent place to start. If a person does not believe the Bible is true, they have no right to say so unless they can prove it is *not* valid. A lot of people spout off at the mouth these days. We have an ignorant generation that believes if they like it, it is true; if they do not like it, it is not true. But when you back them in the corner and demand proof, they don't offer much. They throw out answers like they believe science over the Bible. That is a well-informed group! Science is over-abounding with proof of creation and the birth, life, death, and resurrection of Jesus Christ. And science proves two genders in humanity.

Let's look at the lie people want to believe and use as an excuse when they say they were born a homosexual. Many studies have been completed by scientists, universities, the psychological world, and the medical world. The results still prove that *there is no gay gene.*

In 2019, Benjamin Neale of the Broad Institute of Harvard and MIT published a paper in the science journal. Many people have provided their DNA to agencies that try to find ancestors and ethnic origins. This study, not the first of its kind but the largest, gathered behavioral data from over four hundred thousand people's genetics from the United Kingdom's BioBank study. Seventy thousand individuals submitted to the 23andMe company and agreed their data could be used in research. The study found five genetic variants that could not pinpoint any cause of behavior in same-sex relationships. For example, one variant was related to male baldness and testosterone levels. Another was associated with the sense of smell. The study stated, "We know that smell has a strong tie to sexual attraction, but its links to sexual behaviors are not clear" (McIntosh, 2019).

Fah Sathirapongsasuti, a senior scientist at 23andMe and a gay male, wanted to answer his and others' questions about themselves and the search for a gay gene. He even noted that the most requested information of 23andMe is research and information about sex and sexuality (McIntosh, 2019).

The saddest part of these and many other studies is that people are grasping for excuses for their behaviors. The Creator God gave all the answers we need in the Holy Scriptures, but many people do not want to accept the truth. They want to believe a lie, and many have been given permission to do so.

Behaviors, emotions, and feelings can be controlled and changed. People in these alternative lifestyles, as they tag them, determine their identity by their sexual behaviors. That is *not who they are*. That is *what they do*.

For years, I told women in prison and rehab that sin is a habit. It really is that simple, and patterns can be broken if an individual wants to break them. Any activity or sin can eventually become a habit or sometimes an addiction. People who are in homosexual, transgender, and other deviant lifestyles are living in their feelings and their practices. They have developed a liking for a feeling that they delved into in one way or another.

Some think they cannot change their behaviors. I taught anger management in prison and drug rehab for about twelve years. Without fail, one or two students would raise their hand and present the same lines I had heard for many years.

"Ms. Londa, I can't help it. I just can't control myself when I get angry."

"Ms. Londa, I just black out and can't control myself."

I would reply by presenting a scenario. "Let's say you are in your living room in a rage and in a fight with someone. You cannot control your anger. Then there is a knock at your door, and a voice says, 'Sheriff's Department.' I'm pretty sure you would be able to control yourself at that point." Self-control is a choice and is done on purpose.

I have seen a lot of pre-teens and teenagers declare themselves gay. How do they know? A good friend and an excellent mental health counselor explained that parents need to teach children about their feelings, desires, and emotions when they are approaching puberty. It is fine to have a best friend, but it is not okay to cross a boundary with that best friend and experiment with feelings.

Children do not understand all their feelings, and if they cross a line and experiment with their behaviors, they are told by our culture, "You are gay." No, they are not. They were not born with a gay gene and are too young to understand all they feel and experience. Parents—not the government, the doctor, the school, or their friends—but their parents are the ones who are to mold and develop them. Parents are to guide their children into healthy men and women who understand their sexuality and who understand that God expects them to be good stewards of their bodies. And parents need to be present to help a child who has wandered into the path of deception.

Even Neal's science journal article supports the truth and disputes deception. He explained his team's research and paper:

"We re-wrote major sections [of the paper] to emphasize that the primary focus . . . is on behavior, not on identity or orientation" (McIntosh, 2019).

These researchers call sexual behaviors just that—behaviors. If you are reading this and are in a homosexual or transgender lifestyle, into pornography or any other behavior, try to begin your journey by not identifying yourself by your behaviors.

The world today has adopted the words identity and orientation. Identity is our uniqueness, and orientation is defined as training. So, when someone expresses they identify with a particular sexual orientation, they may not realize it, but they are saying that their unique individual behaviors were learned. A learned behavior in which they were trained. Not a gene, not something they cannot help, not something in which they are doomed to live the rest of their lives.

So, what are we saying? We can search for excuses our entire lifetime to explain our behaviors. Still, the bottom line is that you and I are responsible for our behaviors. We all have seen the typical questioning of three children standing beside their mother's broken dish. When questioned, nobody did it. That is about how ridiculous we appear as adults when we blame our behaviors on genetics, other people, God, and any other excuse we choose.

Stop looking for an identity and be the real person God created you to be. If you go looking for an identity, you will find one attached to excuses. We will stay stuck in our behaviors, habits, and circumstances if we keep manufacturing reasons.

Any psychologist or counselor worth their salt will tell you behaviors can be changed. So why do homosexuals state they cannot change? Simple. It is just like addicts who think they cannot change. The excuses delay the day when one must look in the mirror and say, "I blame no one but you." And on that day, they accept responsibility and seek help to change their behaviors. People who live their lives driven by emotions and feelings live shallow lives.

What about the excuse that God is love and wants us to love any way we desire? I sit and wait for this question. My first response is, "Define love." And I wait. Here is a shocking statement that you may not believe, but in all the years I have asked that question, I have not had one person to date who could give me the true definition of love.

They fumble and bumble around with the "Well, Ms. Londa, I just don't know how to put it into words," explanation.

Then I ask, "How can you base your life and your behaviors on a love you cannot define?"

Let's look at God's definition of love. We call 1 Corinthians 13 the love chapter. It is quoted at weddings, in poems, and in greeting cards. If there is a human alive who can do all this chapter describes as love, they are a saint! Can we endure for a long time? Can we never envy? Can we never promote ourselves? Can we never have pride? Can we never seek our own way over God's? Can we live and never be provoked? Can we never think an evil thought? Can we never rejoice if our enemy falls or sins? Can we stand up and bear all that life deals to us? Can we never fail to love all in all circumstances?

I do not know of a human being that has loved in this fashion and done so perfectly. Love is complicated and requires hard work. Only Jesus has loved in this manner. So, before we say we love God, we need to ask ourselves, are we promoting self and not Him? Are we wise in our own opinion? Are we wanting our way over His?

Love requires the best of us and others. Love requires what is right. If anyone asks you to sin or go against God's Word to prove your love for them, it is not love.

The apostle Paul gave us some examples of love and how it acts in Romans 12 and 13:

Romans 12:9: *Let love be without hypocrisy.*

Romans 12:16: *Be of the same mind toward one another. Do not set your mind on high things, but associate with the humble [low estate, lowly in position and power]. Do not be wise in your own eyes.*

Romans 12:21: *Do not be overcome by evil, but overcome evil with good.*

Romans 13:10: *Love does no harm to a neighbor, therefore love is the fulfillment of the law.*

We all have failed the Lord and sinned. We all have made mistakes. We all have regrets. We are humans who need a Savior. But do we really understand love and love with no hypocrisy? Have you ever read the origin of the English word hypocrite? It originated from the Greek word *hypokrites*, which means "an actor or a stage player." This is a Greek compound word from two Greek words that join to mean "an interpreter from underneath." Greek actors wore large masks, and the actor could be said to have spoken from under the mask (Merriam Webster, Incorporated, 2021).

We can understand more clearly that a hypocrite wears a mask or pretends to be something they are not. True love has no hypocrisy. True love wears no mask. Those who try to change the reality God created are hypocrites who wear masks and pretend to be something they are not. There is hope and a way out, my friend. Seek help in Jesus and ask Him to help you identify with who He says you are. Be oriented (trained) in how to live for Him. If you learn to sin, you can learn to live righteously.

Satan hates God, and because humankind was made in God's image, Satan hates all human beings. We are redeemable. He is not. Satan hates all God is and all that represents Him or reflects Him. No wonder he tries to destroy humankind. If he can twist, warp, and pervert anything that represents God or His image, Satan will. To attack God, Satan must go through His children. He wants to destroy all that displays the truth and glory of God.

Since Satan is no match for God, He aims his warfare at God's children. God created males and females. Satan says let's design many genders. God created man and woman for marriage and procreation. Satan says let's thwart the plan with same-sex attractions and pervert what God created.

All the perversion and alternative lifestyles we see are not a sign of progression. They are a sign of how much Satan hates God and His creation. They are also a sign of the depravity of the mind that can develop when people rebel against a holy and righteous God.

Individuals need to see their behaviors as separate from their identity and call their behaviors what they are: sin! When one views their behaviors as sin and rebellion against God, they can more easily repent, break their habits, and turn from their wicked ways.

In 1 Corinthians 6:9–10, Paul told of sins not permitted into God's heaven. He warned us not to be deceived before the following list:

Neither fornicators, nor idolaters, nor adulterers, nor homosexuals, nor sodomites, nor thieves, nor covetous, nor drunkards, nor revilers, nor extortioners will inherit the kingdom of God.

In 1 Timothy 1, Paul explained that there are sins that are contrary to sound doctrine. In other words, sins that anyone should know are contrary to God's Word and violate holy living:

- Lawless
- Insubordinate
- Ungodly
- Sinners
- Unholy
- Profane
- Murderers of parents
- Manslayers
- Fornicators
- Sodomites
- Kidnappers
- Liars
- Perjurers
- And any other thing contrary to sound doctrine

We cannot isolate sinful sexual behaviors as poor people singled out and oppressed. They are sinners, just like the list of others above who will not enter God's kingdom. The Bible gives many other examples, but it must be understood that sin is sin, and only God is the answer.

I wrote on this subject because sexually deviant behaviors are rampant in the world and places where I have worked. I have seen many people leave their sinful behaviors when they realized they could. Prison is a homosexual culture that is destructive to many. I have seen the light of God's Word dispel the lies in that darkness and set many women free.

If you are reading this and in a sinful alternative lifestyle, I want you to know that God loves you, and I love you. You are not a mistake, and you have value. I want to encourage you to understand that behaviors do not represent who you were created to be and how you are to live. The Bible says all have sinned and fallen short of God's glory. And all of us need a Savior. If you accept that your behaviors are choices and your orientation was how you learned to behave, you can begin your journey to the lifestyle God determined for you. If you are living an alternative lifestyle, chapter 11 in this book will help you understand more about the deception of your sin.

Believers in Jesus have the duty to take the truth to those trapped in the deception of this sin. We must GO and love them and teach them their identity can be in Jesus. Train them (orient them) how to live a life with different behaviors. Sometimes when we GO, we have to teach others how to live apart from the habits and lifestyles they developed apart from God.

5

Watch God Perform Miracles

Don't Look at the E

I was in a season of life quite a few years ago where the Lord was testing and maturing me, even though I didn't realize it at the time. One day a week, I would drive from Lakeland, Florida, to Bradenton to meet one-on-one with inmates all day. The center housed women for the last part of their prison sentence, and they had to work hard to earn the privilege of being accepted into the program. I would leave Bradenton in the evening and drive to Riverview, Florida. I would meet with inmates there in the women's state prison and then go home after leaving the prison at about 8:00 or 8:30 p.m. The round trip was 145 miles.

I woke up one morning knowing my gas tank was empty, and I was at the bottom of the barrel in my bank account. I went out and started my car to make sure, and the needle was on E. That settled it; I would not be going. I went back into the house, and the Lord spoke to me in a manner I cannot deny. I did not hear an audible voice, but I heard it so loud that it may as well have been audible.

"If you do not GO today, the enemy will give you a reason every week, and you will never GO back." That is what I heard resonate through my spirit and my mind. I debated back and forth with these thoughts:

- You do not tempt God.
- You use common sense.
- God gave you a brain.
- Don't put yourself in danger.

Despite it all, I could not get that sentence out of my head, my spirit, and my very being!

It was soon time to leave. No one was around, and I felt foolish. I walked to the car with my Bible and belongings in hand. I got in, put on my seat belt, and said out loud to God, "I am going to obey, but if I get stuck, I am calling a friend, and they better answer the phone!" That was as spiritual as that moment got. I turned the key, and the engine started. *Must have a few drops in the tank,* I thought. I put the car in reverse and wondered how far I could go on E. How would I make a phone call to a friend and explain this? I backed out of the driveway, and off I went.

Was I strong in faith and confident? No! I was afraid. I drove to I-4, one of the most traveled interstates in Florida and in the nation, that would take me to I-75 South. When I got off the ramp and onto I-4, I stayed in the right lane just in case something happened. I was devising a plan to coast off the edge of the road and hoped it did not occur on an overpass. I was not full of might and power. No, I was praying and watching the fuel needle on my old Ford. I was almost begging God to protect me and get me to Bradenton.

The trip seemed like an eternity. I remember when I rounded a corner on I-75 South and saw the Bradenton water tower. I felt relieved and stressed all at the same time. I made it to the center and met with the girls. I told them what had happened and that God loved them so much that He sent me from Polk County, Florida, to Manatee County, Florida, on an empty tank of gas to tell them. We had a great day. When it was time to leave, I had to drive to Hillsborough County to the state prison. I drove the distance, went in, and completed my duties that night for the Lord.

But then it was time to drive home. In the dark. About forty-five minutes from my house. What else could I do? I got in and drove in the night until I got home. I did not tell anyone that story for many years because I wasn't sure they would believe it. You see, we show up and obey, and God performs miracles!

The Card Room

Hillsborough Correctional Institution was a faith-based women's prison in Riverview, Florida. It closed and was torn down several years ago, but I have many fond memories of it and made many lifelong friends there.

In the chapel was a small room that resembled a hallway with a counter and cabinets on one side. It was called the card room because greeting cards were stored in the cabinets, and chapel orderlies distributed them to inmates throughout the year. A door was on each end of the tiny room. One door entered the chapel near the back row of pews, and the other opened into the library.

Women met with female inmates in just about any place you could find space in the chapel for counseling or mentoring. In the entry leading to the library was a small rectangular window. I met with ladies in the card room for one-hour sessions. Often a lady would peek into the small window and wave to let me know she had arrived for her session.

One day, I glanced up as I was finishing with a woman, and another yelled through the door, "Ms. Londa, I'll be right back. I have to go get my belongings."

I waved and said, "Okay." By the time I finished the session I was in, the inmate was back and sitting in the library, waiting for me. Something was off. Something was not right. I told her to come in and close the door. She looked pale, and I knew we had a problem. "What's going on?"

She affectionately called me Sis. "Sis, I don't feel good."

I asked one of the chapel orderlies I knew well to come into the card room with me in case I needed help.

A bizarre coincidence of situations intersected at that moment. What no one knew except the prison staff was that a fake emergency was scheduled that day for training. The team did not know what the crisis would be but expected it that day. The young lady collapsed and almost fell off her chair. I lunged from my chair in front of her and caught her in my arms as she fell. The orderly helped me lift her back into the chair.

"Tell someone to get the chaplain!" I yelled. The orderly opened the library door and dashed to the chaplain's office as I squatted on the floor, held the young lady in the chair, and prayed. I knew the chaplain would call medical. The girl was unconscious. The orderly spoke to the chaplain and ran back into the card room to help me. Neither of us knew that the chaplain thought this was the training emergency. He did not rush but called medical for them to respond to the chapel's card room.

In the meantime, the girl briefly gained consciousness and then fell out of the chair again and onto me. I was now on my knees praying and trying to hold her in the chair so she would not be injured.

"Where is the chaplain? Where is help?" I asked. By this time, a group of inmates and orderlies had gathered in the library. Because I was so focused on the moment, I did not know the ladies were praying and the orderly helping me was praying and checking the girl's pulse.

After a long while, the medical team and several officers entered the library and stood in the doorway of the card room. I immediately began telling them what had occurred, that she was not breathing well and had passed out twice. A nurse very slowly and methodically opened a case and removed a stethoscope. Others just stood and watched as they casually talked. *What is going on?* I thought. This girl has been unresponsive!

I looked at the medical team, who seemed to do very little and talked amongst themselves. I finally said, "Something is not right! What are you going to do? She fell out of the chair into my arms!" They acted as if I was doing well in my part of their planned emergency. I looked at my orderly friend as if to say, "Why don't they do something?" The girl was now conscious again and crying but having difficulty breathing. The minutes passed, and the group just stood there talking. No one rushed.

"What are you going to do?" I asked. I looked up and behind the medical team was one of the best corrections officers on the planet. We all called him O.B. He has since died, but he and I made eye contact. I must have had a look of desperation on my face.

O.B. yelled out, "This is the real thing! This is the real thing!" He ran out of the library, yelling into his radio for someone to call 911. Immediately the medical team and the other officers looked panicked as they realized this was not a training drill. This was a real emergency. Everyone jumped into action.

When an ambulance arrived, which is not common in prison, they put the inmate on the gurney with her yelling to me, "Sis, Sis, don't leave me."

The prison allowed me to run with the gurney and paramedics as far as I could before they took her away. Soon an eerie sound quieted the prison as a helicopter lifted off the parking lot, transporting the inmate to Tampa General Hospital. Evidently, the paramedics had requested a helicopter. We all knew the situation was grave.

I stood at the end of Main Street, which is what the girls called the paved walkway, and felt so helpless. I walked back down Main Street to the chapel and went back inside. The dear orderly who helped me said she needed to tell me something. She had kept track of the young woman's pulse. "Ms. Londa, her heart stopped twice while you were praying for her."

I looked at her and said, "What?"

"Yes, I was monitoring her pulse and her color the entire time, except when I ran to tell Chap, and she had no pulse two different times."

Those women prayed that day in that chapel library. They had no lies to believe. We had told them to trust God in our teachings and counseling, and they did. God met us in the card room that day. I felt no anointing and did not feel God's presence, but I just happened to be there and prayed while others prayed. When the inmate returned to the prison, she received quite a welcome!

The gospel of Jesus Christ works everywhere. In America, in prison, in POW camps, North Korea, Pakistan, India, and anywhere on the globe. The miracles occur when we GO and obey the Lord.

The Men in Black Suits, White Shirts, and Black Ties

In 2005 I went on a mission trip to South Africa with my friend Helen Campbell. We worked there with dear missionary friends, Hil and Leslie Delrosario, who were appointed to South Africa then. We worked out of the Assembly of God church pastored by the Superintendent of the Assemblies of God for Cape Town. The Delrosarios assigned us duties, classes to teach, outreaches, churches in which to preach, etc. As is customary for Leslie, she sprung a few extra surprises on us throughout the trip.

On the last Sunday of the trip, I preached in a church on one side of Cape Town, and Helen preached in another. That evening we were escorted to a church where Helen was scheduled to preach. Leslie was born in the Dominican Republic and is one phenomenal and powerful woman. She gave orders, and we obeyed as you do when working with missionaries.

On the way to the service, Leslie told us the building this church was housed in was owned by Muslims in a Muslim part of town. *Interesting*, I thought. An Assembly of God church renting a building from Muslims in a Muslim-dominated neighborhood. What are the odds? As we approached the church, Leslie told us the truck would pull up to the front door, not to linger outside, but to get out and go immediately into the building.

When I entered the front door, I stepped into a tiny room that served as a vestibule. From there, two French doors opened and led into the space used as the sanctuary. It reminded me of a movie theater. The rows of seats descended, and one small aisle of steps was in the center for entrance and exit. On the floor at the bottom was a small music stand for the speaker, and to the right was the band's equipment.

We all greeted the people. I am a social person, so put me in a room, and I will find someone with whom to talk. Leslie motioned for us to follow her, and we descended the stairs to the front row. The service started, and as usual, I loved the music of the South African churches. Someone introduced Helen, who began preaching. That night an unusual and strong presence of the Lord came into that room. It is hard to describe, but we all knew we were physically feeling His glory.

About three-fourths of the way through Helen's sermon, gunshots exploded outside. I turned and looked at the two doors at the top of the center aisle, expecting men with guns to burst through at any moment. Two strong black men in black suits, white shirts, and black ties stood in front of the doors with their arms crossed over their chests. *They must be security,* I thought.

As the gunshots continued, an unusual event occurred that I had never experienced before or since. I had always wondered what it would be like to be martyred for Jesus Christ. I have read horror stories about how Christians were martyred and hoped I could be as strong. I kept turning and looking at the two men at the top of the stairs. They stood bold and calm and gave off a sense of security. Yet, I was thinking, *We are going to be martyred. I am going to be martyred! I hope my family knows it is all okay.* An excitement flooded me that is hard to paint in a word picture. I felt a bolt of adrenalin and excitement that I had never felt before. Since that day, I have been confident that Jesus meets His martyrs in death.

No one ever breached the two doors. The minute Helen said, "Amen," in her ending prayer, I looked up. The two men were no longer at the door. I turned to Leslie and said, "Where did the two men in black suits go that were standing in front of the doors?"

Leslie looked at me as if I had just spoken another language to her and asked, "What two men?"

"Leslie, the two men who were standing in front of the doors! Where did they go?"

Leslie looked at me strangely again. "Londa, two men were not standing in front of the doors."

I thought if I used charades, she would remember. "You know, they had on black suits, white shirts, and black ties," I said as I ran my fingers from my neck to my waist to show how a necktie would lie. "Never mind." I bolted up that skinny aisle of steps between people. I looked everywhere, and the two strong black men in black suits with white shirts and black ties were nowhere in sight.

On the way back to our rooms that night, Leslie said, "Londa, you saw two angels. No men were standing guard at the door. You saw the angels of the Lord standing guard and protecting us and everyone in that church."

The command for us to GO includes the power and resources we will need when we GO. Taking the step of faith to obey God, and showing up, sets the stage for God to perform miracles and change lives. In those moments, we often encounter amazing experiences.

Go Like Mother

My parents divorced when I was eleven years old, and my mother had been a stay-at-home mom until that time. She worked several jobs for a few years until she opened a residential and commercial cleaning service and became very successful. When I was eighteen, I began working with her and did so for a few years.

My mother believed we could be light to the people who hired us. We received a call for a residential estimate. When we arrived at our scheduled time, we knocked on the door and heard the lady inside yell that she was coming. We waited a while, and when the door opened, the woman was on her knees on the floor. She had crawled to the door and turned and crawled as we entered.

She told us she had health issues and could not walk. When we returned on a scheduled day to begin our work, we found the lady very social and kind. She told us of her faith, which in reality meant she and her husband were in a cult. Over time, she told us more about the cult they were in, and they even had a picture of the guru they worshipped on their living room wall.

Then one day she asked about our faith. The door swung wide open. We began to tell her what we believed from Scripture and kept her in our prayers. My mother told me we needed to continue to love her and talk when she wanted to talk.

We were concerned about her health, but her doctors could not find a cause as to why she could not walk. We knew it was demonic, and my mother decided we would pray over prayer cloths and hide them throughout her house. We anointed several cloths with oil, prayed over them, and took them the next time we went to the home. We pinned a couple of prayer cloths under her bed and others throughout the house. We began praying that God would heal her and make it evident He had healed her.

Time progressed, and the conversations continued about

her cult and our faith in Jesus Christ. We arrived one day, and when the door opened, the woman was standing and welcomed us in. We asked what had happened, and she was unsure. We told her we had been praying for her and had asked Jesus to heal her. She was very receptive and did not doubt what we said.

Not long after her healing, they discontinued our services. We went into darkness, planted seeds, and God did a miracle. We did not have the opportunity to lead her to salvation, but in her darkness, God's light shined brightly.

6

Like Peter and John

There are two types of believers in this world: the religious person immersed in self, programs, and routines, and a servant of Jesus Christ who understands the Great Commission is to GO!

Luke, a physician, wrote the account of the early church in the New Testament book of Acts, also called the Acts of the Apostles. Chapters two and three tell an interesting story that helps us understand our purpose. Acts 2:46–47 says,

*So continuing **daily** with one accord in the temple, and breaking bread from house to house, they ate their food with gladness and simplicity of heart . . . And the Lord added to the church **daily** those who were being saved* (emphasis added).

Notice how the early believers were out and about daily doing what they could. Then we read about a different group in Acts 3:1–7:

*Now Peter and John went up together to the temple . . . And a certain man, lame from his mother's womb was carried, whom they laid **daily** at the gate of the temple which is called Beautiful, to ask alms from those who entered the temple; who seeing Peter and John about to go into the temple, asked for alms. And fixing his eyes on him, with John, Peter said, "Look at us." So he gave them his attention, expecting to receive something from them.*

Then Peter said, "Silver and gold I do not have, but what I do have I give you. In the name of Jesus Christ of Nazareth, rise up and walk." And he took him by the right hand and lifted him up, and immediately his feet and ankle bones received strength (emphasis added).

We see a great contrast here between the actions of the people in the temple and Peter and John. The apostles and believers went out daily and fed people, provided for them, and added to the church. The others carried a crippled man to the temple gate daily and laid him there to beg. Their work was done. They carried him and laid him there for all to see how righteous they were each day, and the man was still crippled and unable to live a normal life and care for himself. He had to beg to eat daily!

Both groups were busy daily but did not follow the Lord's mandate. What we do daily matters.

Ever since I was a teenager, I have enjoyed reading about the late Mother Teresa, a missionary in Calcutta, India. She once said,

By blood, I am Albanian. By citizenship, an Indian. By faith, I am a Catholic nun. As to my calling, I belong to the world. As to my heart, I belong entirely to the Heart of Jesus" (Mother Teresa Center, n.d.).

Do we see our heart as belonging to Jesus and our calling to the world? I think Peter and John knew this before Mother Teresa.

Just Follow a Simple Bit of Advice

I once worked at the Peninsular Florida District Office for the Assemblies of God. The best boss I ever had was at that job, Superintendent Terry Raburn, and his wonderful wife

Athena, my dear friend who passed away three years ago. I had been working at the district for several years when a job opportunity as a counselor in a drug rehab for women was presented to me in a rather sudden way. I spoke to Terry Raburn for advice, as the job required me to be on duty every Sunday. I will never forget his words, which were divine directions for my life: "Londa, this is your ministry. Go!"

There was that word: GO! And GO I did. One of my best friends, Michele Mitchell, whom I had served with side-by-side in prison ministry for many years, was the chaplain in that center at the time. Michele ended up in an office on one end of the building, and I was in an office on the other end. We were like bookends in the hallway. I cannot tell you how many women we were able to pray for and lead to salvation in our offices. Counselors were not allowed to share their faith unless a client asked. But when a client asked, I was careful to take as long as it took to answer the question.

People, in general, want the truth. In my classes, group therapy, and private sessions, sometimes a client would ask a question that could be answered more correctly from Scripture. I would say, "Do you want me to answer that as a counselor or as an ordained minister?" In all my time at that center, I never had one client answer that question, "As a counselor." One hundred percent of the clients answered, "As an ordained minister." It may have taken the rest of class to answer the question, or it may have taken an hour in my office, but God opened a way to GO amid a worldly system.

That program was rough, and we had to stand up and fight in spiritual warfare daily. Michele told me that sometimes God puts His people in places to restrain and hold back evil. Believe me, I have seen it face-to-face. We had to find ways to help the women and be a light in the darkness. The women were up by 5:00 or 6:00 in the morning and did not go to bed until late at night. Their days were full. When they reached phase two of the program, they had to find employment while keeping up with their program and therapy.

Because they were in drug rehab, the agency adopted the stance that if the women were sick or in pain, they were drug-seeking. Not always. Life happens. I watched some of my clients reach the point of exhaustion and have trouble functioning. They were malnourished and sleep-deprived from drug abuse before being court-ordered into the program, and many had health problems.

The little sleep and stress of the program, and the rehabilitation from drugs, were sometimes overwhelming. A counselor could call a client out of any class, group, or setting and could not be questioned as to why. I would try to watch my clients, and when one was sick or exhausted, I would call them to my office at the beginning of a group or class.

"Why am I here, Ms. Londa?"

"Close the door."

"Okay.   "

Then they would turn and look at me with a puzzled look on their face. They didn't understand why I called them to my office when they did not have a scheduled one-on-one with me.

I would reply, "You aren't feeling well, and I have a lot of paperwork to do. Just lay down on the loveseat and take a nap. I'll take you back to where you need to be when we are done with this session."

To some of the women who were sick, fevered, or sleep-deprived, that forbidden nap on my office love seat meant more than anything else I could have done for them. Jesus talked about giving a cup of cold water to a thirsty person. People need to know someone cares.

The Major's Office

I was sitting on the front row in a faith-based prison chapel service when a guard tapped my shoulder and said the major wanted to see me in the chapel lobby. I thought I was there for the Sunday service, but God thought otherwise. I walked into the hallway where the major was waiting and asked if she needed me. She informed me the prison had received word of an inmate's mother's death and had confirmed it according to the Department of Correction's protocol. The chaplain was not on duty that Sunday, so the major called me out of the service to deliver the news.

Of all the tragedies I faced over the years, these situations were never easy. Since the chapel was full of inmates and their families for the service, the major told me to come to her office, and she would have the inmate report there. Being called to the chaplain's office is scary in prison because it can mean you will be receiving bad news. I wondered if the inmate would think she was in trouble by being called to the major's office.

I walked with the major to another building and into her office with my Bible in my hand. I prayed and asked God to help me. The young woman came in and was scared that she had been called to the major's office. I sat down beside her and talked with her, gave her the bad news, and stayed with her as she cried and grieved. That was not an easy day. My purpose that day was not to be in a chapel service but to be with a young lady in the major's office to give her some of the worst news of her life.

Peggy

I met with a young woman in prison before her release. I was attempting to help her find a safe place after the end of her sentence to receive the help she needed. She asked me to telephone her Aunt Peggy in Texas as she was the one person she trusted and loved above all others. Peggy had always been there for her and cared for her when she was small and when her parents did not. I called Peggy one evening and introduced myself, and we discussed the plans for her niece. I learned that this story would turn out completely different than thought.

I liked Peggy immediately! She was a comedian in her own right and genuinely loved her niece. She offered information that helped me as the days progressed with her niece. The niece was released from prison and quickly faded from contact with me and her Aunt Peggy. However, my friendship with Peggy grew, and with Peggy in Texas and me in Florida, our phone calls evolved to three or four times a week. Peggy became one of my dearest friends. Long trips on the road were filled with conversations with Peggy.

Peggy had severe health problems, and I always told her I was praying for her. She never missed a Christmas or birthday, and a box always arrived at my door for each. The most significant event of our friendship was that Peggy became a servant and friend of Jesus. She began reading the Bible, and though I never met my dear friend face-to-face, we shared a close bond. We had pictures of each other and always said we would get together one day in Texas.

Peggy's faith and relationship with Jesus grew as her health declined. As the years went on, our calls were less frequent as her energy deteriorated due to her sickness. And then it happened. I could not reach her and did not hear from her. I tried to get information and finally turned to the internet. There it was—Peggy's obituary. My heart was broken at the loss of my friend.

Peggy could never attend church because of her health, and our church occurred in phone conversations. I look forward to the day I enter eternity. I will meet one of my best friends face-to-face and in perfect health. We can visit as much as we want. And we will laugh. I'm sure lots of laughter is in heaven around Peggy, my dear friend who met Jesus outside the church's walls. I'm so thankful I took the advice of a young girl in a Florida prison and called her Aunt Peggy in Texas one evening on an ordinary day.

Hank

My grandmother lived with me as her Alzheimer's began and progressed. Grandma was four feet tall and had lost some height since her younger days when she stood four feet and eight inches. The day Grandma and I moved into our duplex, we moved across the street from Hank and Lois, who we did not know but would become dear friends and part of our family. They knocked on the door the day after we arrived, and we invited them into our pile of furniture and boxes. Hank asked if we needed help with anything and said he was a Jack-of-all-trades and master of none. He fixed a lamp for me, and from that day forward, he and Lois were always available to help.

Hank was a truck driver and drove from Florida to New York and back each week. Lois had retired and was always available to help with Grandma. As was Grandma's manner, and now in her eighties, she wasted no time to find out if Hank and Lois were ready to meet Jesus. Lois was much farther along than Hank, and he was a little stubborn. He was a big tough man with a heart as big as Montana, but he was a softy when it came to Grandma. The two became like mother and son—the son she never had. Grandma and I eventually moved four miles up the road, but our relationship with Hank and Lois deepened. Hank helped us move and was always there anytime we needed him.

One Saturday, Hank and Lois stopped by on their way home from errands. The four of us sat in the living room, and Hank told us he was seeing a doctor when he got back from the next week's run. He was not feeling well and was in pain. Grandma wasted no time talking to Hank about eternity. He finally looked at me and said, "My brother is an Assembly of God preacher on the east coast of Florida." Yes, I about fainted, but Hank was beginning to talk. Lois was incredibly supportive and never pushed Hank.

Hank was scheduled for tests when he went to his doctor's appointment. The results came back and shocked everyone. Hank had pancreatic cancer that had moved into his liver. The doctor gave him six months to live. It was like receiving news about a beloved family member.

Hank spent a week or two in the hospital, and one day Grandma asked me to call his room and hand her the phone. Grandma sat down in a chair and talked to Hank. I listened as she gave him the gospel message in her own words. Grandma told Hank her life story and how her parents were not Christians, but she wanted to be saved at a very young age. She had that desire inside. A friend of hers invited her to church with her family when my grandmother was about ten years old. She was so excited and planned to give her life to Jesus that day, as she did not know how and was sure she would have the opportunity in a church.

Grandma sat in the pew, waiting anxiously for the moment she would be a Christian, but the preacher did not give an altar call that morning. She did not know what to do, so she went home sad and disappointed. She continued telling Hank how she met my grandfather in her early teens and married him the night she turned sixteen. Marrying Grandpa was the pathway that led to the opportunity to accept Jesus as her Lord. Grandma shared the Scriptures with Hank and in her own words told him to ask the Lord to forgive his sins and believe in the Lord, and he would be saved.

Shortly after that phone conversation between Grandma and Hank, I stopped by the hospital one evening to visit him on my way home from work. Lois had gone home for the day, and I thought he was tired and had only planned to stay a few minutes. However, he asked me to sit down and visit with him. Hank brought up the phone conversation between Grandma and him and wanted to talk. We talked for about two hours, but he did not surrender his life to Jesus.

Hank came home, and Grandma kept after him. He loved Grandma about as much as anyone, and her loving words softened his heart. Eventually, a hospital bed was moved into the living room. The big tough truck driver was declining and had become a thin and dying man. I was at work one day at the Assemblies of God District Office when my cell phone rang. I saw it was Lois and answered. She told me I needed to come to see Hank alive. I told her I would be right there. I ran into my boss's office, Superintendent Terry Raburn, and told him my neighbor was dying and was not ready to meet Jesus. Could I please GO and pray with him.

"GO!" was his answer.

Everywhere I work, I keep a Bible on my desk. I grabbed

my Bible and belongings and ran to my car. Lois had told me that Hank was unresponsive, and the medication made him sleep. "Londa, don't be surprised if he doesn't know you or respond to you," she had said.

Before my brain registered what I was about to say, I blurted out, "He will!" I immediately wondered why I had said that.

As I drove, I called my friend Michele Mitchell, and she prayed that God would wake Hank and give him the opportunity to pray with me. I also called Grandma, and she told me what to tell Hank on her behalf.

I pulled into the driveway and went to the back kitchen door. Lois met me at the door and again said, "Don't be surprised if he doesn't respond." Lois' niece, a CNA, cared for Hank at the house. Her children, who were like grandchildren to Hank, were there along with Lois' daughter. They led me through the house to the living room. Hank lay in the hospital bed and was unresponsive.

I pulled a chair close to his bed, laid my Bible on the bed, and said, "Hank, we don't have time to argue! You are dying and Grandma told me to tell you that she is old and will not live too much longer and wants to spend eternity in heaven with you. Now Hank, we don't have time to argue and put this off any longer! You are going to pray with me. You are going to repent and accept Jesus as your Lord, and you are going to die and go to heaven!"

Hank's eyes opened. He turned his head toward me, smiled, and reached out his weak, thin hand. I grabbed his hand and began praying. I didn't realize the family had come into the room and surrounded the bed. When I finished praying, I looked up with Hank's hand still in mine, and the entire family was crying. Hank drifted off again after we prayed, and I stayed for about an hour. Before I left, I walked to the foot of Hank's bed, where he appeared to be asleep. I gently grabbed his toes through the sheet and said, "Hank, I'm going home now. I love you, and I'll see you in heaven." Hank opened his eyes, smiled, and drifted off again.

Early the next morning, Hank opened his eyes and motioned for the children to come close to his bed. He smiled and waved at them and stepped into the presence of Jesus. To this day, Lois is part of our family, and we all know we will be together in eternity with Hank.

Ms. Audrey

I lived in one of four apartments in a small building in the antique district of town. The first neighbor I met was Marilyn Pitzer, a Baptist Mid-Mission's missionary and Bible translator. Marilyn worked in the jungle in Argentina for years, translating the Bible into the Warao (*Wad-ow*) language. Marilyn worked with the Warao Indians for decades and then moved into the city where she continued to translate the Bible. When she and I met, Marilyn and her coworkers had translated enough books of the Old and New Testaments that a dedication of the Warao Bible was planned. Due to the takeover of Maduro, the decline in the country, and its quick fall to socialism, Marilyn and other missionaries were forbidden to reenter the country. They continued the work from afar.

Marilyn and I became great friends and because we are both pet people, she spent a lot of time visiting my pets. Our small apartment building shared a common front porch. In the first apartment was Ms. Audrey. She was old, frail, in poor health, and smoked like a chimney. Over the years, when home on furlough, Marilyn had made efforts to share the love of Jesus with Ms. Audrey.

Rosa, our other neighbor, was a Christian, and we all worked together to check on Ms. Audrey and help her when we could. One day I knocked on her door to check on her, and Ms. Audrey asked me if I could unscrew the top on her orange juice. From then on, I became the remover of lids. Rosa cooked often and took food to Ms. Audrey, and Marilyn and Ms. Audrey developed a code to alert us if we should be alarmed. If Ms. Audrey's newspaper was not taken in by a certain time of day, Marilyn knew to GO in and check on her.

As Ms. Audrey's health declined, we became more concerned about where she would spend eternity. She had been quite unkind to Marilyn on occasions and made it clear she did not want to hear the gospel. Hospital visits became more frequent, but Ms. Audrey instructed the hospital staff that Marilyn was the one person they could speak to on her behalf. She asked Marilyn to call her one living relative, who lived very far away, in the event of her death.

Then the last hospital visit came. Marilyn was now working from home as a Bible translator, had flexibility in her schedule, and could GO to the hospital daily. And she did. Marilyn and I would talk every evening for an update. Ms. Audrey could no longer speak but would shake her head back and forth to say, "No," each time Marilyn asked to pray with her. Marilyn prayed anyway. One evening, Marilyn informed me that the hospital staff did not think Ms. Audrey would last through the next couple of days. She asked if I wanted to GO with her the next day, which was a Saturday.

"Yes! I want to GO," I said.

When we arrived at the hospital, the nursing staff said Ms.

Audrey would be moved to palliative care later in the day to wait for the moment of death. Marilyn looked at me, and we both knew this might be the last chance for Ms. Audrey to accept the Lord as Savior. We entered the room and saw the tiny and frail Ms. Audrey swallowed up in the bed. She saw us and smiled. We stood close to her bed, with Marilyn on one side and me on the other. We spoke with her for a few minutes.

We knew time was limited. Marilyn shared Scriptures and explained salvation again, and Ms. Audrey seemed uninterested. When Marilyn asked if we could pray with her, Ms. Audrey pressed her lips together, and slowly moved her head from one shoulder to the other to communicate, "No!"

I immediately blurted out loudly, "Why not?"

I guess that shocked Ms. Audrey, and she looked up at me. I leaned down to make sure she heard me. "Ms. Audrey, I don't know what the hospital staff has told you, but you are dying. You may not live until tomorrow. Now we do not have time to argue. You are going to die and step into eternity any minute. Marilyn and I want you to spend eternity in heaven with us. We love you and want you there with us."

Ms. Audrey looked at us like she had nothing else to offer. Marilyn took over and prayed for salvation. When we were ready to leave, we told Ms. Audrey we loved her and hoped to see her in heaven. As we went around the foot of the bed toward the door, I looked back. Ms. Audrey smiled and blew me a kiss; I returned one to her.

Neither Marilyn nor I know if Ms. Audrey believed in Jesus that day as her Lord, but I hung on to the smile and the kiss as we left the room.

Ms. Audrey died the next day. I know the Lord gave her that time with a faithful missionary who would not give up and was relentless in her attempts to see a lonely older woman enter eternity with Jesus.

Buster

His name was Buster, and he lived across the street from my grandparents. Buster was an alcoholic. As his alcoholism progressed, his health declined. He reached a point where he called a taxi to deliver alcohol to his house every day. My grandmother had befriended Buster and his sister and tried to help them. She looked for an opportunity to introduce them to Jesus.

I received a call one day from my grandmother. She had not seen Buster or any activity at his house for several days. Because she had the spare key to his place for emergencies, she went in and found him unconscious. An ambulance took Buster to the hospital, and he was admitted. He had diabetes, and because of the lack of care from drunkenness, Buster's toes had turned black and were rotting off his feet. He was dying and would not come home. Grandma asked me to take her to the hospital and said we had to GO and pray for Buster because he was not ready to die.

I was young and had not become a minister at that point. Preachers were allowed into the rooms, but not just anyone could walk into intensive care. My four-foot grandmother didn't care what the hospital thought. She was on a mission, and we were not leaving until we prayed with Buster.

We entered a small area where there just happened to be five or six pastors who walked into that small space at the same time. We barely had room to move. A nurse asked where each was going and then looked at Grandma and me. She asked if we needed help, so I told her we were there to see Buster.

"Are you family?"

I looked at her and said, "This is my grandmother, and Buster is her neighbor. We want to pray with him and won't stay long." For some reason, the nurse said okay and pointed us to his room.

We walked into the room where Buster lay in a coma. Grandma lifted the foot of the sheet to show me his dead black toes. Grandma stood on one side of the bed and I on the other. Grandma began talking to Buster and telling him how much the Lord loved him and how to be forgiven for his sins and enter eternity. She said, "Now Londa is going to pray for you."

I looked at her and nodded my head as if to say okay. Then I looked down at Buster, held his hand, and said, "Buster, if you can hear me, and you want Jesus to be your Savior, and if there is any way at all you can let me know, please let me know now." Immediately Buster's head turned toward me, and he blinked his eyes three times. I prayed and asked the Lord to forgive his sins, save him, and take him into heaven when he died and left his body. After the three blinks, there was no more movement or response, but I knew Buster had heard me. Shortly after those few moments, he left that dying body and entered heaven as a new creature.

We must take an honest and in-depth look at ourselves, our motives, our service to God and man, and how and why we do what we do. I want to GO and act as Peter and John did and realize my call is to the world. I GO because my heart belongs to Jesus.

7

Tell the Truth

In February of 2005, Florida was stunned by the abduction and death of Jessica Lunsford at the hands of John Couey, a convicted sex offender. Couey kidnapped nine-year-old Jessica, held her captive over that weekend, raped her, and then killed her by burying her alive. I remember watching the news story and can only describe the gamut of emotions as horrifying.

The week after the news broke in Florida about Jessica's shocking ordeal and death, I went to a Florida State prison to counsel women. The women were waiting with the question, "If God is a God of love, why did He allow that monster to kidnap that little girl and bury her alive? Why didn't God stop him, Ms. Londa? Why?"

I was as appalled as the women were at John Couey and wished they would place him in a male prison yard and announce to the inmates that the guards were turning their backs for thirty minutes. I knew that would not happen, but it was my secret wish for justice for Jessica.

I said, "I don't know why God did not rescue that little girl, but I can tell you this: If God intervenes and stops all evil, then He will remove humankind's greatest power, our will. If God takes away our ability to choose, then we are robots and puppets. God did not create us to be robots but to be His children.

We get to choose to love Him, trust Him, and obey Him."

I cannot even guess how many times I have been asked that question over the years. My answer is always the same. The one thing God will not touch is the human will with which we say, "Yes, God, I will serve you," or "No, God, I will not serve you." It also leads to the fact that we as believers must pray, intercede more, and push back the forces of darkness with the light inside us.

I once sat in a small room with a sobbing young woman who had just received news her brother had shot himself while she was incarcerated.

"Ms. Londa," she said. "Is my brother in hell? I have to know. Is he in hell?"

I replied that I did not know if her brother was in heaven or hell. I told her that the spirit enters eternity and that even when the body is shutting down, I believe the spirit can call out to God, who hears and accepts that repentance. "If your brother cried out to God from his spirit, then God accepted him into His presence. You and I do not know if he did that, but I hope he pulled on what was instilled into him throughout his life. We don't know, but I want you to know that the spirit can call out to God."

One evening, I received a phone call from a young lady I met in prison and helped her upon her release and beyond. She was extremely sick and not doing well.

"Ms. Londa, if I sleep with my boyfriend and die in my sleep, will I go to hell?"

I replied, "I can only say if you have to ask that question, there is probably a reason. I would not take the chance if I were you." She died not long after that phone call.

"You know, Ms. Londa, I can't work, but if need be, I will get a side hustle. I will do whatever I have to do." This I have heard multiple times over the years.

My reply is, "Really? You can prostitute or sell drugs, but you cannot get a job?" These women had every excuse as to why they could not get a legitimate job, and they believed the lies they were telling me.

"You know," I said, "You can get a job. You can go to school. Other people do it. Why can't you?"

As they mumbled, "I don't know," or gave another excuse, I would say, "The first step is the hardest. Just do it and quit making excuses!"

I have heard many reasons and met many people who have believed many lies, including their own. It is a sad way to live. A life built on lies has no solid foundation. A foundation of sand provides no strength for people to get their footing and to create a productive life.

Just tell them the truth.

When I worked in drug rehab, counselors had to guard against grandeur thinking in our clients. It is common in addicts and criminal thinking. "I like the needle. I am addicted to the needle." Or "I like to cut myself and feel the pain and the blood running down my skin."

Mental health conditions often need to be addressed in these situations, but some people like to use shock value and make everyone think they are the worst. My answer remains the same: "I don't care if you like it or not. Stop it! It is time to get help and change your life."

I remember a young woman in prison who was near the end of her sentence and had a young daughter waiting for her at home. This young woman was a cutter, which is not the best habit to have in prison. One evening she did not show up for class, and I asked where she might be. In prison, you must be where you are supposed to be at all times. "Ms. Londa, she cut herself really bad, and they had to take her outside to a hospital in Tampa."

I learned that this young woman found some object and cut her abdomen open from one side to the other. She was in the hospital and had surgery. I also remember the first night of class when she returned after her long ordeal. The women were walking into the class, and I was standing outside the door, greeting them and talking. I saw her coming. I was so excited to see her and was happy she had lived and was recovering. As inmates filled the classroom, I waited to speak with the young girl. She told me how she was doing and said she did not think she could stop cutting herself. She knew she was going home soon but stated she was addicted.

I did something that night that I had never done before. I realized later that the hand of God was involved in what seemed crazy at the time. As I heard that young girl who had nearly killed herself say she did not know if she could stop, I grabbed her shirt collar and moved her into the corner right inside that classroom door. I held on to her shirt as I pressed her against the corner of that room and said, "Do you want your little girl to do this?"

She looked at me in horror and said, "No!"

Still clenching her shirt, I said, "You either need to stop it or get professional help. If you do not, your little girl is going to want to do what Mommy does, and how are you going to handle that? Or are you going to kill yourself the next time and leave her permanently?"

I let go of her shirt and realized I was thankful no guards had walked by. The girl looked at me and said, "I don't want my daughter to ever experience what I have gone through."

I looked directly into her eyes and said, "Then either stop it now or get help immediately!"

If any counselors are reading this, you may be experiencing anxiety. Thankfully, this story ends well. That young woman was released from prison, went home to her daughter, and quit cutting herself.

I realize my words and grabbing a young girl's shirt collar cannot change her. But I know God does not work in our list of checkboxes. I was at a point of desperation that night as I realized this was life and death. I do not know what that girl heard, saw, or felt, but God brought change to her when a woman grabbed her shirt and shoved her into a prison classroom corner and spoke the truth. God delivered her in a most unusual manner.

I will call her Angela. She was a beautiful young woman I met in a prison, and I attended one-on-one sessions with her for a long time. She left her husband and children at home. Angela was endearing. She had big, beautiful eyes and a smile like a little girl that captured your heart immediately. Angela could also be the ditzy blonde at times, and I had fun with her and some of the other women. Angela worked through many issues while incarcerated, and the day came when she went home to her family. Her daughter was young at the time and needed her mother.

Angela came to my ordination in 2013 with another friend from prison. I will never forget how the ordination class lined up in a huge church building in central Florida. We had a long trek to walk through the hallways before entering the auditorium. We rounded a corner, and Angela walked straight toward me in a bright red dress.

"Angela? Go that way!"

I also noticed that Angela wore a pair of extremely high-heeled shoes, and I knew the girls called them hooker shoes. It seemed out of character for Angela. I later learned that as she walked to her car to drive to the church, the heel broke off her shoe. Her only pair of dress shoes. There was only one store between Angela's house and the church, and she discovered the only types of shoes that the store sold were hooker shoes.

Angela would not miss my ordination and bought a pair before heading to the church. Angela made the situation comical in her red dress and hooker shoes and didn't even realize it. Our friend teased Angela all evening about her hooker shoes. One of the funniest parts of the evening happened at the end of the service, as we were all gathered at the altar after the ordination candidates were ordained. I saw Angela and her friend looking at the shoes of church ladies with looks on their faces that seemed to say, "Look, she has on hooker shoes too!" It is not the norm at ordination, but it's a great memory we have always chuckled about.

In May 2020, I received a message on social media from one of the ladies in prison at the same time as Angela. It was a devastating message. Angela had been murdered! I looked up the local news articles, and it was true. She was murdered and taken from her family. I was shocked. We never know what tomorrow will bring. We live each ordinary day and go about our day. I don't think the greatness is in preaching to the masses but daily going where our destiny leads us for those twenty-four hours. Many times Angela and I talked through challenging situations in her life. I looked directly into her eyes and told her the truth, and I will never regret those times.

A few years before Angela's death, I stood at a funeral home with Angela and two other ladies who had been in the same prison with her. We were attending the funeral of one of the ladies' fathers. I still have the picture of the four of us behind the funeral home. We never expected that Angela would be murdered a few years later, and the one whose father died would die a few years before Angela.

Life is delicate, serious, fragile, and unpredictable. By not going to people daily, we take a risk we cannot afford. The greatest sermons are the daily lives we live. We all fail at times. We all fall short. We all sin. We are not perfect. We all have strengths and weaknesses. But God does not anoint the perfect. He anoints the obedient. We all must repent at times and walk through lonely and tough places. The gospel is getting up every day and doing what is on our plate for that day. Being faithful to God, true to ourselves, and telling the truth to others.

My friend Suzann and I enrolled in a college course in photography when I was working in children's ministry. We did a lot of design and printing for the church and decided a photography course would enhance our abilities. We attended the course at a local college in Tampa that was a very liberal school but had a good photography course.

I loved puppetry and had mastered the voices and characters of nine puppets I used in children's ministry. We were given an assignment late in the semester to capture defining moments and show who we were. This assignment had to include a large display of photographs we took, developed, placed on a matboard, and would be displayed for our presentation and critique in class. The course was right before photography went digital, so we did all our developing in the darkroom on campus.

A young girl in the class made it known she was a lesbian, and she did not believe the Bible. Throughout the course, Suzann and I tried to be kind to her. When working on projects, this girl often asked us many questions about God and the Bible. She was also very outspoken and critical.

One morning I was in the darkroom finishing a project prior to a 7:30 a.m. class when that young girl entered to complete her assignment. She began asking me questions about my faith and attempted to criticize me. I was kind to her and spoke the truth to her. She finally did not know what to say and backed off.

On the day of the presentations, we each had to display our photos in our designated spot in the classroom. When the teacher called upon a student, they gave their presentation, and then the class critiqued the display. My project included shots of our puppet ministry, puppet dramas in children's crusades, and me surrounded by all the puppets whose characters I created.

Suzann also had some shots of one of our children's crusades titled "Garbage In Garbage Out." Our team built a dumpster that served as the home for two puppets, Ralph and Elmer, during the dramas. Suzann's presentation was before mine, and the class was very involved and interested in her presentation. She fielded many questions and received an excellent score. Suzann was able to speak openly about the gospel and her photos.

My turn came, and I was unsure of the response I would

receive as my presentation was completely puppets with outreach and crusade photos. I did my presentation, answered questions, and sat down. The professor then stated she was delighted by our two presentations, as puppetry was art, and we were in the art building on campus. The professor then asked me to come back to the front of the class and explain more about a couple of my photos.

The photos the professor pointed out were part of a children's crusade where leaders presented the plan of salvation. I stood before the class in a secular, liberal college and explained the plan of salvation as illustrated by the puppet photos. The response was wonderful from the class and from the professor.

On the ride home, we talked about how we were amazed at the door God had opened and the response from students and our teacher. The lesbian girl who had bombarded us with questions and criticism throughout the class changed toward us after that day and became a friend. We then had more opportunities to speak freely with her and share the love of God.

We cannot be trapped in the mentality that ministry is only on a platform or in front of a crowd. Ministry is opportune everywhere we GO daily.

8

The Good Samaritan Days

GO! What does it really mean? How do we do it daily and not just on Sundays? Jesus told the story of a man that journeyed from Jerusalem to Jericho and was attacked by thieves. They beat him, took his clothes, and left him exposed to the elements and dying. The story is in Luke 10:31-37:

Now by chance a certain priest came down the road. And when he saw him, he passed by on the other side. Likewise a Levite, when he arrived at the place, came and looked, and passed by on the other side. But a certain Samaritan, as he journeyed, came where he was. And when he saw him, he had compassion. So he went to him and bandaged his wounds, pouring on oil and wine; and set him on his own animal, brought him to an inn and took care of him. On the next day, when he departed, he took out two denarii, gave them to the innkeeper, and said to him, "Take care of him; and whatever more you spend, when I come again, I will repay you." So which of these three do you think was neighbor to him who fell among the thieves? And he said, "He who showed mercy on him." Then Jesus said to him, "Go and do likewise."

Let's look at some key elements of this story. The Samaritan was not the only person who came upon the man who had been robbed, stripped, beaten, and left to die. He was the third person whose path intersected with this man. This seems to say we will all encounter opportunities in our days, but only certain people will take the time and suffer the inconvenience to do something.

Imagine how the man felt. He was beaten and injured, and as he realized someone had seen him and walked away, he must have felt hopeless. Jesus said the Samaritan had compassion. This was not the actions of the priest and Levite, who may have thought the situation was sad. Compassion is action. Compassion can lead to work, inconvenience, money, and time, and this man did just that through his actions.

The Samaritan poured oil and wine into the man's wounds to cleanse, disinfect, and bandaged them. He provided the practical need for medicine. He then placed the man on his animal and provided transportation to an inn. He offered a place of safety and convalescence and paid for his time there. Jesus taught that this is being a neighbor and followed this teaching with the command to GO and do likewise.

Years ago, I was working on the staff of a church in central Florida, and I had to arrive at the church very early on Sunday mornings. Each week I passed through an intersection about half a mile from the church where a convenience store was on my left. One Sunday morning, I pulled behind a pickup truck to wait for the red light. The passenger door opened, and the male driver pushed the woman in the passenger's seat out of the vehicle. She looked around as the summer Florida sun beat down on her and walked toward the store's parking lot.

The light turned green, and the pickup truck disappeared as he quickly drove off. I placed my foot on the gas pedal and proceeded toward the church when God spoke to my heart and said, "Go back and pick her up." I reasoned within my head that I would be late, she might be dangerous, and several other reasons. The impression got louder and stronger. "Go back and pick her up." I finally could not fight it any longer and made a U-turn and drove back to the intersection and into the parking lot of that convenience store.

I parked and entered the store, and the woman was nowhere in sight. Great! I thought. I should have just obeyed the first time I heard go back. I finally asked an employee if he had seen the woman and described her. A man who was shopping heard me and said, "She's standing out there," and pointed to the sidewalk in front of the store. She must have exited after I had entered the store. She was dirty, smelled horribly with body odor, and looked lost. Not knowing what to say, I approached her and said, "Hi."

She looked at me, the stranger, and cautiously said, "Hi."

"I saw you get out of the truck in front of me at the red light and thought maybe you needed some help."

No reply. This was going great.

"Look, I know I am a stranger to you. I work at the church down the road. If you want to go with me, I can get you something to eat. Are you hungry?"

She was, and off we went. We kept cereal, milk, and other food in the church kitchen for kids we bused in from low-income areas. I gave her breakfast, introduced her to several people, and had my team cover for me in the children's ministry so I could sit with her in the service.

After the service, I inquired where she wanted to go, and she asked me to take her to a friend's house. I talked with her in the car and gave her my cell number.

For the next three months throughout that hot summer, I kept water and snacks in my car, as it seemed four out of every five times I left my house, I saw her walking the streets. I would pull over, roll down the window, and say, "Get in. Where do you need to go today?" I gave her water and food and transported her around town. Each ride gave us opportunities to talk. After those three months, I never saw her again.

I was supposed to help her and plant seeds in our car talks. I also recommended agencies that could help her. But she was a good lesson and test for me. It would have been a lot easier to pass by that Sunday morning. I drove out a lot of gas in those three months, but my car sermons were hopefully watered by someone else. She needed Jesus, but she also required practical needs met.

That was a Good Samaritan moment. These kinds of moments we happen upon. They are not planned, nor are they convenient. There are many moments like this in our weeks and months, but we must act in compassion or pass by.

I pulled into a gas station/convenience store one day as I was working and was standing at the gas pump, filling the tank. This establishment had a fast-food type of restaurant inside, and round tables were outside for patrons. I glanced over and saw a woman sitting at one of the tables crying. By her feet was a large plastic bag like the ones in which people's belongings are placed when they leave jail. I continued pumping, and then there it was—that same impression as the day I turned around and took the prostitute to church. I knew the rest of my day would be miserable if I did not obey. Trust and obey and GO.

I put the gas cap on, and the parking space in front of her just happened to be free. I pulled in, got out of my car, and walked over to the table where she sat with her head on it.

"Excuse me. Do you need help?" She looked up at me, wiped her tears, and said, "I just got out of jail, and I can't walk any further." She had walked about eight miles at that point and was out of steam. It was a hot day in Florida.

"Where do you need to go?" I asked. She needed to go to the opposite side of town to get home. "Well, I know I am a stranger, but if you trust me, I would be willing to take you."

We got in the car and drove the distance across town. Of course, I had a captive audience and had time for a car sermon. I told her I had been in prison ministry for many years and had been in jail many times. She needed resources, so I wrote down some contacts and gave her my cell number. I never heard from her, but I did my part. I obeyed the command to GO.

My friend and her husband conducted a homeless ministry for a period of time in the parking lot of a venue. The ministry grew, and before long, many people gathered to be fed, receive resources, and hear the gospel. Many accepted the Lord, and the ministry was growing every week.

The venue where they held services and fed the people had recently been recarpeted. One Saturday during the homeless outreach, a Florida storm blew in, and a downpour of rain fell from the sky. My friends were going to usher the people into a large multipurpose room to feed them and continue the service, but the manager put a quick stop to the plan.

The reason? They would get the new carpet wet and dirty. In other words, lay them at the gate like the crippled man but do not bring them inside. We don't want to get our hands or our carpet dirty. The rain and storm that day presented a Good Samaritan moment, but that man blew it as he was more concerned about the new floor covering than he was about the homeless people in the parking lot.

In my early teens, we lived one mile from my grandparents and rode to church with them each week. On the way, we passed a homeless man every time we drove down Main Street to the church. One day my grandmother looked at my grandfather and said, "We are going to help that man." We stopped and met him and found out he had lost his job, fallen on hard times, and was homeless. He had used drugs and had many problems, but he was on the streets and needed help. When my four-foot grandmother made up her mind about something, no one changed it!

This story was one of the greatest lessons I have ever learned about living the gospel. I watched my grandparents, over time, purchase a small trailer, furnish it with used furniture, and supply it with food before we moved Bill into his new home. It was a gamble, but Bill jumped on the opportunity. He found a job, cleaned up his life, became productive, and found purpose again.

For years as I was going through high school, it was not unusual to stop by my grandparents' house and see Bill sitting and visiting with them. Bill was grateful for an opportunity to live life again. He remained faithful to working and visiting my grandparents for years until an opportunity opened for him to move away and better himself.

Bill's life was saved, and Grandma ensured she gave him the gospel message. Many people drove down Main Street where Bill was living, but my grandparents realized the opportunity could not be missed.

Reading through the gospels, we see more recorded about Jesus outside than inside the temple. He knew He had to GO to the people. People were healed and changed everywhere He went, and many miracles happened in the lives of those He encountered.

We see God perform miracles in the midst of going to change the lives of people. Here is an example from Matthew 9:32–33:

As they went out, behold, they brought to Him a man, mute and demon possessed. And when the demon was cast out, the mute spoke.

In Matthew 20, Jesus encountered two blind men sitting beside the road, begging Him for help. He healed them. Jesus could have walked by. He could have acted as if He did not hear them amid the multitude.

In Matthew 28, Mary Magdalene and the other Mary went to the tomb while the men remained in hiding. They encountered an angel and an empty tomb, and Jesus met them as they went to tell the disciples.

Jesus went to the house of a Pharisee to eat on the Sabbath in Luke 14. This was an invite He could have easily turned down. Jesus knew every word and every action of His would be scrutinized and questioned, but He went. Because He went, a man was healed of dropsy.

The ten lepers were healed in Luke 17 as they went because Jesus went to Jerusalem.

These were Good Samaritan days. They were unplanned and unexpected, and each could have been avoided or an excuse given to ignore them.

Do not be misled. I have passed opportunities. I can think of one Good Samaritan moment I missed because I was busy and had no money that day. To this day, my heart is grieved when it comes to my mind. We all have missed opportunities, but let us determine to obey our Lord and GO when He presents the need. Proverbs 16:9 says, "A man's heart plans his way, but the Lord directs his steps."

This verse describes the flow of life with God. God directs our steps to GO on Good Samaritan days.

9

You Don't Have To Be Perfect

I have had my share of heartaches in life. My only brother died in 2004 at forty-two, and it was a difficult road of grief. My parents had divorced when I was eleven, and I grew up in a single-parent home. I was born with foot problems, have encountered many surgeries, and have difficulty finding shoes. We all encounter struggles. Life is not easy.

In rehab we taught the girls they had to face life on life's terms. I have seen too many people die from drug overdoses, and still, to this day, I get the word about the death of a former client in rehab. In the adoption field, we buried an abandoned baby. I preached at the funeral, and my boss was the attendee.

This work of the gospel is not for the faint of heart. It is not for the insecure or cowards. Sometimes we walk together, and sometimes we walk alone. There is no compromise of God's Word in the gospel. The gospel stands alone. It has always stood victorious over those who tried to disprove it.

Our deepest and darkest days build strength and courage in us. I cannot trust a God deeply whom I have not known to bring me through the darkest of nights. Ecclesiastes 7:14 explains that God appoints days of prosperity and days of adversity and that we would be arrogant if we knew all that was in our future:

In the day of prosperity be joyful, but in the day of adversity consider: Surely God has appointed the one as well as the other, so that man can find out nothing that will come after him.

I remember when my brother Doug died in April of 2004. He went into a coma on my birthday and died two days later. I remember those days vividly each year. Three months after Doug's death, I was scheduled to lead a team of twenty-six people to conduct a kid's camp in Abaco, Bahamas, for one week. I was still grieving, and my heart was broken. I was not sure I could make it, but I went anyway. We had a wonderful week and witnessed God do amazing things in the children and in our team. I was learning 2 Corinthians 12:10:

Therefore I take pleasure in infirmities, in reproaches, in needs, in persecutions, in distresses, for Christ's sake. For when I am weak, then am I strong.

This verse is part of a discourse where Paul explains a difficulty for which he could not find relief. Paul had received a vast amount of revelation from the Lord, and he had tremendous responsibility on his shoulders. So he wouldn't become arrogant, and so others would not see him as anything other than the man he was, he stated the following in 2 Corinthians 12:7:

And lest I should be exalted above measure by the abundance of revelations, a thorn in the flesh was given to me, a messenger of Satan to buffet me, lest I be exalted above measure."

Paul did what anyone would do. He prayed and asked God to deliver him from his suffering: "Concerning this thing I pleaded with the Lord three times that it might depart from me" (2 Corinthians 12:8).

But God's response was not what Paul expected: "And He

said to me, 'My grace is sufficient for you, for my strength is made perfect in weakness'" (2 Corinthians 12:9a).

Paul then stated how he would proceed:

Therefore most gladly I will rather boast in my infirmities, that the power of Christ may rest upon me. Therefore I take pleasure in infirmities, in reproaches, in necessities, in persecutions, in distresses, for Christ's sake. For when I am weak, then am I strong (2 Corinthians 12:9b–10).

I cannot say that I boast in infirmities. Who enjoys sickness or pain? I have also heard many sermons throughout my life and read various writings of what others suggest was Paul's thorn in the flesh. Some propose poor eyesight, his short stature, or sickness. I personally think it was what he said in verse 10: infirmities, reproaches, necessities, persecutions, distresses, and weakness.

A messenger of Satan buffeted or struck Paul with various attacks. Paul described this as a thorn in his flesh. If you have ever had a splinter in your finger, you know it can be a nuisance, but the piercing of a thorn is quite painful! This messenger of Satan attacked Paul in his flesh, body, and human nature with its frailties and passions. Throughout Paul's life, this messenger brought many attacks. Let's look at each one.

- Infirmities involve lacking strength, illnesses, and feebleness in the mind or body.
- Reproaches are the insults, injury, hurt, and harm others can bestow upon us.
- Necessities are imposed by external circumstances or internal pressure.
- Persecution means to be harassed, primarily because of a person's religious beliefs.

- Distresses are seen in the narrowness of a room and anguish. In other words, when we are crushed or when things are closing in on us.

Paul said when he was weak, which meant diseased, sick, or lacking strength, then he was strong (Blue Letter Bible, 2021).

Paul understood that the mandate to GO meant to do so daily. He had plenty of excuses, but even when sick or imprisoned, he knew his strength did not come from himself. That is the key. Paul knew the One whom he believed and trusted, and his strength came from Jesus.

We seem motivated to GO and do when all is well and when we feel spiritual and close to God. When we find ourselves being struck at every turn, we give every reason why we cannot GO. If we fall or sin, we beat ourselves up and give in. Sometimes those distressing times come, and the stress and pressures feel like the walls are closing in on us. But Paul is an example of one who learned to keep going and doing in all circumstances, whether he felt like it or not.

Friend, be encouraged if someone has told you that you have sinned or lack faith if you experience difficulties in your life. Look at Paul's example. His life shows us that we will be tested, tried, and experience sickness and problems in this life, but we must continue with endurance. Proverbs 24:10 says, "If you faint in the day of adversity, your strength is small."

In Thessalonica, Paul and Silas had to leave for their own safety because they had caused such an uproar in the city by sharing the gospel. Acts 17:6 says, "Those who have turned the world upside down have come here too."

When you must leave a city for your safety, you may not

feel like you are turning the world upside down, but we cannot base our actions on feelings. I taught the women in prison and rehab that feelings come and go, fluctuate, and change. Our feelings even lie to us at times. If we base our daily lives and behaviors on emotions, we will never be stable. We GO regardless of how we feel. We GO because it is our purpose and the right thing to do.

I met a young woman in a Florida prison who surrendered her life to Jesus and experienced a positive change. When she arrived at the prison, there was a shortage of uniforms. She was issued clothes that were much larger than the size she wore. To make matters worse, she lost weight in prison and had to work to keep her pants up because belts are not part of prison uniforms, for reasons you can imagine. The woman did not have much money given to her for canteen or clothing, as her family could not afford it. She had been learning about prayer and became quite a prayer warrior.

Twice a year, the women could order items from a catalog, such as underwear, shoes, long underwear for winter, and T-shirts. The final day to order was approaching, and she still needed money. Inmates were not allowed to place orders unless their account had enough money to cover the costs.

This young woman came into the chapel one day to a meeting we were conducting. She said she had a testimony, and we asked her to share. She had prayed and told God she needed clothes and underwear that fit her. She felt prompted to go to the canteen, get in line, and place her order. The young woman struggled, knowing she didn't have enough money in her account, and feared she would be punished for placing an order for which she did not have the funds.

The prompting continued, and when her turn came, she placed her order and waited for the account total. She was told the amount in her account, precisely what she needed to buy the clothes and items she ordered. God miraculously put the money in her account. Sometimes we GO in fear as we obey a prompting.

That young woman learned what Paul taught. Life's situations may seem impossible or rough. Money may be sparse, but GO when God says GO, and He will perform the miracles. That woman's testimony encouraged a chapel full of women, and others began to trust God for their needs. And that is sometimes the purpose of our challenges, that others may see and be encouraged to GO and do likewise.

We are fooling ourselves if we wait until we feel like it, when circumstances are accommodating, or when we think we are at a spiritual height. Look at the men Jesus called to be his twelve disciples. They were less than perfect, but Jesus saw their potential and knew they could fulfill their purpose in this life with all their imperfections and failures.

I remember one Saturday morning when I was teaching classes with my friend Sharon Guedry in a maximum-security prison. Sharon had another commitment that weekend, and I headed out early to travel to the prison to teach our class. I was more tired than usual that day and had one of those weeks, as we all do from time to time. I began to pray in the car as I traveled on the interstate. God's Spirit visited me in the car that day, and His presence was so intense I seriously thought of pulling off the road but knew I would be late if I did.

As I drove, I prayed, cried, and interceded. At one point, I wondered what people might think if they glanced over at me as they drove past. At the same time, I did not care. This intercession lasted a long time, and finally, it began to ease.

I looked in the rearview mirror at my teary eyes. I thought, *Well, I'll have to do something about myself before entering the prison.* I did not know what lay ahead that day, but I knew God had strengthened me when I was weary and prepared me to GO into the prison.

The class was small, and I pulled desks together to make one large rectangle we could sit around. This presented a more intimate setting for the women and me to communicate. Directly across from me sat a woman who had only been in prison a couple of years and had a life sentence. She was a "lifer." She informed Sharon and me at the first class that she was unsure if she believed but would listen and hear us out. I told her, "Fair enough."

We were about twenty minutes into the class when a very young girl who sat to the left of the lifer began disrupting me. I respectfully looked at the young girl and instructed her to stop. She continued, and to my surprise, the lifer intercepted the situation for me. The lifer told the young girl to stop, show me respect, and pay attention. If she did not, she would deal with the young girl when they returned to the dorm.

Time out for an explanation. Prison is the lifer's home. Everyone else is visiting for a while. Some lifers do not change, but many do and become great role models and attempt to help younger people change their lives. When a lifer corrects a situation, you better listen. They have nothing to lose, and intelligent people take heed.

The young girl immediately sat up, paid attention, and showed respect. The lifer then asked me a question, and I answered it with Scripture and an explanation. She then opened up and told some of her story, which can make a person vulnerable in prison. She had lived over fifty years and then committed murder. She had recently lost a dear family member. She was grieving and could not forgive herself for the actions that removed her from her family and the one she loved so dearly.

God opened the door for me to minister to that woman that day, and she listened with an open heart. I was so glad I drove that trek early that Saturday morning when I was tired and pushing myself to GO. When I am weak, Jesus remains strong!

As we go about our day, employment, and responsibilities, we should realize that we are involved in the Great Commission every moment. It is part of who we are and what we do. It is our lifestyle and how Jesus lived and walked on this earth. Acts 17:28 says, "For in Him we live and move and have our being."

We do not GO because we are perfect. We GO because our Lord commanded us to GO. In Him, we live and move and GO!

10

Be the Light Bearer

We cannot talk about our duty to GO daily without understanding the spiritual warfare involved. Satan will not just sit back and lose souls without a fight. Humans will be involved in our war, but our battle is against the forces of darkness.

Ephesians 6:12–13 says,

For we do not wrestle against flesh and blood, but against principalities, against powers, against the rulers of the darkness of this age, against spiritual hosts of wickedness in the heavenly places. Therefore take up the whole armor of God, that you may be able to withstand in the evil day, and having done all, to stand.

"That you may be able to withstand" means to stand against, i.e., to oppose and resist. Verse 13 finishes by saying, "and having done all, to stand." The word *stand* means "abide, continue, establish, stand up, and stand by." In other words, in the fight against evil, the Word of God and His armor give us the strength to stand against evil and continue to establish God's work and kingdom. It is often tricky, and the battle gets intense, but we must stand our ground (Blue Letter Bible, 2021).

In the prison system, when inmates are moved from solitary confinement, and often for other reasons, they are bound in shackles and moved from point A to point B by guards. Other inmates are not permitted to be in the path in which the inmate will be moved to protect the one in shackles.

If you have never seen a person in shackles up close, it is a vulnerable position. The person is bound around the waist, and the chains connect to their wrists and ankles. When they walk, they shuffle due to their ankles being bound. You can hear the shackles with each step. A guard holds on to the inmate's arm throughout the process, and the person is most vulnerable while in restraints. The prisons know if a shackled person is attacked; they have no defense in their vulnerable state. Therefore, other prisoners are locked in their appointed place at the time of the shackled person's movement.

When Hillsborough Correctional Institution was open, it was a faith-based prison that God used for His work during that season. There were times I would walk down Main Street and see a prisoner in shackles surrounded by guards walking toward me. I would stand aside and not move until the inmate and guards passed. We followed this protocol if we got caught in the pathway of a shackled woman being escorted. It was for the safety of the individual but also to lessen her fear so that the guards knew we were respecting the situation.

Seeing shackled women is a sight that, once you observe the fear and shame in their faces until they are unshackled, you will not forget. That fear, vulnerability, and the inability to defend themselves is a picture of the bondage people live in daily in this world. We have the key that unlocks the shackles, but we often have to walk the vulnerable road to reach the destination. If we see ourselves as that guard, holding the person's arm as we walk with them, armed with weapons as we move to a safe place and can free them from their shackles with a key, we see how to walk as we GO daily.

We are vulnerable at times. Our enemy is nearby. At times others want to destroy not only us but also the ones we are rescuing. Like the guard with the authority and radio, we have our armor to make it to safety.

Hillsborough Correctional Institution mainly relied on Christian groups that volunteered to run the various programs. This faith-based initiative tested how this model would reduce the recidivism rate in the state. Many women left that prison and succeeded in life, and the recidivism rate lowered. However, as the battle in the spiritual realm intensified, the desire to keep it open failed as the state eventually closed it. (Park, 2004)

Many women in Hillsborough Correctional Institution learned the power of intercession during spiritual warfare. God did amazing things in that prison, and I hold those memories dear. I was in the chapel one day, and one of the prayer warriors came and said she needed to speak with me. The woman said a large black figure walked through their dorm at night, and she had seen it. She wanted to know what she and the others should do.

I told her and several other ladies about a prison I read about in another country full of gangsters, Satan worship, and murders. It was so dangerous that the prisoners ran the prison. The gospel spread in that prison because someone decided to GO. The men were saved, tore down their satanic altar, grew food, and fed the local community.

The women in Hillsborough Correctional Institution were challenged by this story. They began to form a twenty-four-hour prayer barrage against the attacks from evil forces. It worked like this: At 10:00 p.m., a lady in bunk five would pray for one hour. At 11:00 p.m., she would tap the lady in bunk six, who would cover the next hour and so on. Only those who wanted to participate did. We also had to figure out a way for the women to anoint the dorm, as anointing oil was contraband for an inmate to possess.

"Do you have anything you can use as anointing oil?" I asked.

They did not, but the black girls used pink oil to moisturize their hair. "Would a bottle of that work, Ms. Londa?"

"Why not? Can someone buy a bottle at canteen that we can pray over and use it only as anointing oil in your dorm?"

The women were on it, and the next time I arrived at the prison, the ladies proudly presented me with a bottle of pink oil that we prayed over and asked God to anoint. I instructed the prayer warriors how to pray: to anoint every part of the dorm and pray Scriptures and command that black being leave the dorm and never come back in the name of Jesus! And they went on a mission! That evil being left and was never seen again. The women were also encouraged to know God heard their prayers and delivered them from a satanic attack.

The enemy attempted to intimidate the women who were growing in their relationship with God by a dark figure walking through their dorm at night. Intimidation is a weapon the enemy uses in spiritual warfare. We must remain diligent to immediately chase it off when we realize what is happening.

If you are wondering about the pink oil, one of the black girls kept it in her footlocker. She was proud to be the keeper of our anointing oil; no one in the prison knew the difference. When you GO and do God's work, sometimes you have to be creative.

When you are involved in situations where people are set free from Satan's grip, your life will not be a bed of roses. Attacks will come in ways you might not recognize, but ones that beat you down, injure, and hurt you. People can be cruel and attack the reputation of the Lord's servant. One may get discouraged and another criticized by those who see every weakness and fault. Go anyway! They did not call you, and they did not rescue you from sin as Jesus did.

Go despite opposition. We cannot seek or depend on the approval of man. Depression, loneliness, financial woes, sickness, and many other challenges can come our way to beat us down and stop us. We will experience seasons of rain and seasons of drought. Sometimes we can sense and feel God's presence, and other times we feel distant and can only put one foot in front of the other. Don't stop. Continue to GO!

We must learn to fight in the dark. Psalm 18:11-14 explains how God does this:

He made darkness His secret place; His canopy around Him was dark waters And thick clouds of the skies. From the brightness before Him, His thick clouds passed with hailstones and coals of fire. The Lord thundered from heaven, And the Most High uttered His voice, hailstones and coals of fire. He sent out His arrows and scattered the foe, Lightnings in abundance, and He vanquished them.

God knows how to maneuver in the darkness and use it for His advantage to launch surprise attacks on the enemy. We see in Psalm 18 that God hid in darkness, ambushed the foe, and scattered them. Satan and his minions are not omniscient, and often God will move us under cover of night. Acts 23 reports the events of Paul's near flogging with the plot and oath of more than forty Jews to kill him. The night before they made their oath, Jesus spoke to Paul:

> *But the following night the Lord stood by him and said, "Be of good cheer, Paul; for as you have testified for Me in Jerusalem, so you must also bear witness at Rome."*

God allowed Paul's nephew to hear the plot and report it to the commander, who then sent Paul to Felix, the governor. In verse 23, the commander orders the soldiers to transport Paul "at the third hour of the night." Even the ungodly know that a good soldier uses the cover of night to outsmart his enemy.

The women in the prison that chased off that black figure learned to outmaneuver the enemy in the dark. Their pink oil, the prayer chain throughout the night hours, and the name of Jesus were a surprise attack the enemy did not see coming. They learned to turn on the light and extinguish the darkness. Amos 6:1 warns those who are at ease or sleep in the dark: "Woe to you who are at ease in Zion."

Our greatest weapon in the darkness is turning on the light. Nothing can dispel darkness like light. I had a client in drug rehab who spent most of her growing-up years with addict parents, and her bedroom was the back seat of a car. She was a beautiful young girl but uneducated in many simple life skills. As her counselor, I had to teach her to brush her teeth a minimum of two times daily. She would come into my office, sit down, and begin to talk. I would look at her when the odor of her breath hit me and say, "Did you brush your teeth today?"

She would respond, "No, I forgot."

Proper hygiene was a program requirement, and the girls had shower caddies in which they kept all their hygiene products for shower time. As we sat in my office, I explained how she needed to take her caddie to the bathroom every morning and at night at shower time. While in the bathroom, she needed to brush her teeth. The look on her face told me the light had been turned on, and she now understood. All these years later, I still hear from her from time to time, and she has made life accomplishments.

When God came out of that camouflage of darkness we read about in Psalm 18, I think He burst out with the power and brilliance of His light to defeat His enemies. This became real to me in 2006 while on a short-term mission trip to Taiwan. One assignment of mine was to teach a group of children in a Buddhist culture about Jesus. I asked the missionary for guidance and will never forget her reply: "You have to tell them why Jesus is different from all their other gods. If you ask them if they want to accept Jesus, they all will. He is one more idol to set on the shelf and worship."

The Buddhists worship thousands of false gods and spend their lives in fear, trying to please and appease their gods. The day of the class for the children came, and we were prepared with a multitude of visuals. I taught about the birth, life, death, and resurrection of Jesus. I told the children why He came and died. But the light was turned on when I explained how Jesus is different from all other gods for two reasons. He is the only God that loved us enough to die for us, rose from the dead, and is alive; we serve Him because He loves us, and we love

Him. I could read it on their faces. They now understood why Jesus is the only God who loved us and gave His life for us.

Second Peter 1:19 says,

We have also a more sure word of prophecy; whereunto ye do well that ye take heed, as unto a light that shineth in a dark place, until the day dawn, and the day star arise in your heart.

The "day star" in this verse refers to the light bearer (Blue Letter Bible, 2022). We carry God's light inside us, and when we walk into the darkness, we cannot help but shine.

I walked into a maximum-security prison one Saturday to teach a class. The major, who was in charge of all security in the prison, was walking toward me. I needed to ask her a question. She was obviously upset by something that had occurred before my arrival. I told her good morning and asked for her instruction regarding my inquiry. I never had any issues with her and always treated her respectfully. In response to my question, the major leaned into my face with my back against a wall and yelled at me in front of the inmates.

I listened to what did not make sense but knew she was obviously taking her frustration off what had occurred earlier. I could read the face of an officer standing behind the major, who seemed to say, "I am so sorry."

I clenched my Bible to my chest and opened my mouth to reply but saw a vision. A hand appeared in front of my face and moved from left to right like a windshield wiper. Everything in front of me where the hand swiped turned brilliantly white. I couldn't even see the major's face or think of one word to say. She stopped talking, and we just turned and walked away.

I went to my class, still baffled about what had just occurred, and could make no sense of it. The only thing I was sure about was that God stopped my mouth. From that day forward, the major treated me with respect and kindness. To this day, I don't know what she saw. I do know God shined the light in that dark moment, and I believe that light did more for the major than I will ever know.

On another occasion, I entered a prison. Standing in front of the chapel was a woman named Natalie who said, "Ms. Londa, can I talk to you?" She explained she was getting out in one week, had nowhere to go, and had no one outside who would be capable of helping her. The chaplain had instructed her to speak with me.

"One week is not a lot of time. Couldn't you have talked to me sooner?" But something about Natalie tugged at my heart, and I knew she was one I needed to help.

"Let me make some calls and see what I can do."

I got her into a program, and from that program, other steps transpired. Natalie was determined, and we shared a lot of tears and laughs. When she would get emotional, I would say, "You'll be fine." Eventually, that became a joke between us. When Natalie faced any struggles, she said to me, "I'll be fine."

The pivotal moment came for Natalie when someone trusted her, gave her a chance, and told her, "You'll be fine." Natalie eventually graduated college, secured her own home, and works full-time in her industry. We are still friends, and she holds a special place in my heart. When she stood on the chapel steps the day I met her, I could see the fear on her face and the darkness that surrounded her. Natalie was full of talent and potential. She just needed the light of God's love turned on to reveal her ability to succeed.

We are called to GO to darkness as light bearers who walk into the darkness and turn the light on. When the light is turned on, it is amazing what we see and what those in darkness see.

11

Uncover the Truth Exchange

My grandmother used to say, "You can want something bad enough that God will let you have it. Israel wanted a king, and He gave them Saul." We all know that Saul became trouble to Israel and was not God's chosen king.

I have sat with women in prisons who all shared similar stories:

"I knew I shouldn't have gone with that dude that night. Had I not, I wouldn't be an accomplice to murder. But I wanted the drugs."

"I lived almost half a century and then wanted my own way, and now I am in prison for life."

"I knew when I ran out of the house I shouldn't get in that car because I had too much to drink, but I didn't care. I was angry and wanted my way. Now I sit here in prison and live with the guilt of the baby I killed in that wreck."

"I wanted my boyfriend and the drugs so bad that I helped him mutilate that girl."

"I didn't want anything to interfere with my drugs and

partying. I had six abortions. How do I deal with the guilt?"

"I was high and nothing else mattered. I threw my baby down the steps, and now I can't live."

These statements portray stories I have heard over the years from women who wanted their own way, and it cost them everything.

Romans 1 describes the progression of deceit and sin and how people reach a point where they exchange the truth for a lie, as we read in verse 25:

Who exchanged the truth of God for the lie, and worshiped and served the creature rather than the Creator, who is blessed forever. Amen.

It is possible to exchange the truth for a lie. Remember that Satan does not care which lie we believe as long as we fall for one. Deceit is more than being tricked or believing a lie— it is replacing or exchanging the truth with a lie. When we do this, we fall into idolatry. We exchange Almighty God's place in our life with a lie, and the lie we believe becomes our god, our idol. But there is a problem with idols. They are not real. They are not the best. They are a substitute. They are false, and they fail us.

Several years ago, I met with an incarcerated woman who killed her baby violently and tortuously. The details are too horrible to mention. How does a young woman get to that point? It is not natural. It is not human. It is not even how animals treat their babies, so how does a human murder her baby? God put an instinct into women to protect their children at any cost. Somewhere the truth was exchanged for a lie, and the lie became an idol that eliminated its victim. Behind every idol is a demonic power whose goal is to destroy its victims.

When I volunteered in the prisons, I met many other volunteers who were Buddhists, Jehovah's Witnesses, Unitarian, and Wiccan, along with many wonderful Christian people. One of the Buddhist volunteers and I were at the prison simultaneously, and I got to know her well. She was a wonderful lady and a kind person. It bothered me that she had exchanged the truth for a lie. I began praying for her and also for the women attending her classes.

I was in the chapel library one day, and one of the orderlies pointed to a plastic tub and said, "Ms. Londa, do you know what that is?" I did not, and she moved the tote closer to me and removed the lid. Inside was an idol the Buddhist volunteer had brought for her sessions. The chaplain was a good Christian man, but chaplains cannot deny any inmate their religious belief, so his hands were tied except for his intercession.

On another day, I was sitting in the card room with Shannon, who has become a dear friend over the years, and while volunteering in the prison was one of the strongest intercessors I knew. I leaned my arm on a plastic tote sitting beside my chair.

"You do know what that is, don't you?" Shannon asked.

I glanced at the tote and said, "Is that the idol?" It was. I took the lid off and peeked at the idol wrapped in cloth. The two of us decided we needed to get the idol out of God's house before the ladies exchanged the truth for a lie.

"Can you get the pink oil, so we can anoint this thing and get it out of here?" I asked Shannon.

"Of course, I can!"

My next visit was an idol removal mission to prevent the

women from exchanging the truth for a lie. Shannon had secured our pink anointing oil, and she and I met in the card room. It now served as the idol's home when not set up for Buddhist classes in the library. Most of my private sessions occurred in the card room, and I found it interesting that the idol landed there when not in use.

Shannon and I anointed the idol with oil and decreed that its power was broken, and no one would be deceived by it. We asked God to remove it from the prison. Within a short time from that day, I noticed the tote with the idol was missing. I asked Shannon what had happened to the idol. She smiled, shrugged her shoulders, and said, "It's gone." We did not know where it went, and we never saw it again.

I met an incarcerated woman who stated one day, "Ms. Londa, I've decided to become an atheist." She looked at me, awaiting a response.

I replied, "Okay, but why do you want to be something that doesn't make any sense?"

She did not want that response and asked, "What do you mean?"

"Why belong to a group that fights against something they believe does not exist? If God does not exist, why label yourself, expend your energy, and fight against Him?"

The conversation was going differently than she wanted, but I continued. "If you are going to belong to a group that takes a stand, why don't you join a group that doesn't waste time fighting something they say does not exist?"

That woman was trying hard to exchange the truth for a lie. It was my duty to tell the truth. I continued to explain to her the facts that prove the birth, life, death, and resurrection of Jesus. When I asked for her facts, there was a deficit.

I entered Hillsborough Correctional Institution one evening with a group of volunteers headed to the chapel, classes, or private sessions with inmates. One middle-aged woman and I were cleared through security at the same time and walked into the first building together, which was the administration building. From there, doors entered the compound.

I had seen and spoken to this woman many times and assumed she was a Christian. I told her what I had read in the book of Luke that morning. When she and I entered the administration building lobby, a guard told us an incident had happened on the compound. We needed to remain in the lobby until he told us to proceed to our classes.

We sat down in the lobby chairs facing one another and began talking. The woman asked what type of employment I had and what classes/work I did in the prison. I explained my job and ministry and then asked about her affiliation. She told me she was affiliated with a group I consider in opposition to the gospel and God's Word. I was excited, as I had never had a face-to-face conversation with someone of this belief. We were locked in a room in a prison, so this would be an interesting conversation, as I was eager to speak the truth.

"What does your church believe?" I asked.

"We accept everyone," she said.

"What do you mean by everyone?"

She lit up as she explained. "We accept Muslims, Buddhists, Wiccans, homosexuals, Christians, and just everyone. We judge no one and accept any faith or belief."

"I see. What do you believe about eternity? Where do you think you will go after you die?"

The look on her face changed to less confident. "We hope there is something after death, but we just are not sure."

Interesting, I thought. "Are you really willing to base your entire life on earth and your eternity on something you are not confident of?"

"Yes, I am."

"Not me," I said as I held up my Bible. "God's Word tells me about my purpose on earth and where I will be in eternity. I don't have enough faith to live my life based on something I cannot prove or that I am unsure even exists. Are you willing to do that?"

"Yes!"

I looked directly into her eyes and the answer to my next question was unexpected. "Are you happy?"

I have to tell the story exactly as it happened. Behind the woman's blue eyes, I saw two dark eyes slide from her right and look through her eyes. She opened her mouth, and a deep, growling voice snapped, "Yes! I'm happy!"

Immediately the guard entered the lobby and said, "Ladies, you can go to your classes now." The woman hurried to leave my presence. I knew that woman had exchanged the truth for a lie and had been deceived by a demonic power controlling her. How sad that a wonderful woman was living and basing her eternity on a doctrine she could not prove while unsure of her eternity.

I began praying for that woman, that God would set her free and not allow her to teach that truth exchange to the ladies in the prison. My custom was to put anointing oil on my head, hands, and feet before entering a prison. I kept it in my car and applied it to my hands before exiting my car, as I usually saw her at the guard shack where we checked in through security.

I made a point to pat her on the back or arm and speak to

her each time I saw her and prayed for her under my breath. I also asked God to prevent her from teaching falsehood to the ladies. After a few weeks of those prayers, I never saw that woman again. I only hope my light in her darkness was brightened by others as she journeyed further.

One day after an appointment with a birth mother with whom I worked in the adoption agency, she said, "I thought I had my pot covered up with perfume, but the doctor knew it anyway."

"Yeah, the smell is quite strong, sweetheart."

"It is?"

"Yes, you can't fool too many people with pot and perfumed mixed together."

"But Ms. Londa, I have to use it because it calms me."

"Why not just take your medication the doctor prescribed?"

"But the pot helps."

I looked at her and said, "Where is your Bible? You used to tell me you were reading it, and you used to talk more about God."

She dropped her head. "I lost it."

"You lost your Bible?"

"Yes, ma'am."

"Then we need to get you another one."

I tried to talk with this young mother and many like her who had exchanged the truth for a lie and believed they could not function without drugs, alcohol, or an abusive man. The scary part about the truth exchange is that it leads to destructive or dangerous avenues. Remember the young woman in chapter 1 who believed she was mentally disabled and was not?

She had exchanged the truth for a lie, and her entire life before the day we met in my office was based on a lie. When we enter the truth exchange, we deceive ourselves.

First Corinthians 3:18 says, "Let no one deceive himself."

If humans did not engage in the truth exchange, our prisons and drug rehab centers would be empty. I have never met a woman in either who had not taken the path of the truth exchange that led to incarceration or rehab.

Mark 8:37 says, "Or what will a man give in exchange for his soul?"

This verse explains the purpose of the truth exchange: to exchange the truth for one's soul. An exchange is a trade of one thing for another. This was Satan's purpose all along when he introduced deception in the garden of Eden.

As Christians and those who know the truth, how do we help others deceived by the truth exchange? One of our duties as light-bearers is in how we live.

Exodus 20:7 says, "Thou shalt not take the name of the Lord thy God in vain." When we think of this command, we assume we should not use the Lord's name in swearing and evil speaking, which is true. But it is only a part of the definition of the word *vain*, which includes the following: "Emptiness, vanity, falsehood, emptiness of speech, lying, and worthlessness of conduct."

Our conduct and how we live daily matters to God. In Ecclesiastes, Solomon discussed vanity and certain actions being vain. Throughout the chapter, Solomon used the Hebrew word *hebel*, which we have translated as "vanity" and "vain," and is defined as "empty." "Vanity of vanities, saith the preacher; all is vanity" (Ecclesiastes 12:8).

Hebel comes from a root word, *habal*, which besides meaning "to be in vain in act, word, or expectation," also means specifically "to lead astray and to make or become vain."

Our life, actions, and endeavors can be in vain, and we can lead others astray. When we GO and shine light in the darkness, we dismantle the truth exchange by not living our lives in vain. We cannot show disrespect or ineffective actions toward the Lord's name, which involves all His character and who He is. People trapped and deceived in the truth exchange need to see the truth in individuals whose lives are meaningful and in opposition to vanity.

If Solomon had written after the cross and resurrection of Jesus, he might have written more about not allowing our daily lives to be lived in vain. He would have encouraged us to make every moment of every day worthy of our Lord.

When we GO, our responsibility is to help people see how the truth exchange has occurred and progressed in their lives. Part of our duty to GO involves turning on the light of God's truth in the darkness of the truth exchange.

12

In All Seasons

Ecclesiastes 3:1 explains that life progresses in seasons: "To everything there is a season, a time for every purpose under heaven."

In Genesis 8:22, notice God's promise to humankind after the flood: "While the earth remains, seedtime and harvest, cold and heat, winter and summer, and day and night shall not cease.

God made life move within seasons in nature and our daily lives. We have all experienced a season we did not want to leave. It may have been a good time of life, or leaving the season may look as if we will lose something essential to us or even people we love. But when the season is over, the season is over.

Can you imagine someone living in the northern United States who refuses to admit summer is over? They continue to mow their lawn in the fall, then pull the mower out of the garage in January and drag it out to the snow-covered yard. They pull the cord to start the mower. That person is going to experience trouble, setbacks, and frustration. We cannot move forward in a season while we are holding on to the previous season with all our might, or if we are trying to function in the new season as we did in the old. I'm confident a mower pushed through the snow will experience mechanical problems.

Years ago, I was a children's pastor. When that season ended, I worked in prison ministry and as an associate pastor and returned to college. I then entered a season of working in drug rehab and, from there, to the adoption world. This is not the totality of my adult life, but each season has had different responsibilities, challenges, battles, and victories. Each season had unique people, opportunities, and methods. But all were God's purpose. I have experienced seasons where I traveled regularly and seasons where my duties did not require traveling. Each season was unique and had its purpose.

Problems arise when we tightly clinch a season in our hands and refuse to let it go. We miss opportunities when we do not let go of what is behind us. Holding on to the old season weakens us because we strive to maintain something that is completed. As a result, we exhaust ourselves.

Part of the deception of this fear is that if we let go of our comfort zone, we will be alone and never have relationships, love, and opportunities as we had before. Fear is the driving force behind this type of action. The weakness from the strain of trying to hold on to and revive what once was makes us weary for battle. The enemy can take advantage of this. We can't see what's ahead because we are looking backward, like driving a car while looking in the rearview mirror.

As a caregiver for an elderly parent and grandparent, I have had seasons of acceleration and seasons of rest. None was more spiritual than the other. All were in God's purpose.

We cannot compare our current season to what season others might be in at the time. People often miss seasons in God's purpose. The new season is not what they want or think it should be, so they return to the old season and become trapped in the past. Their wheels are turning, but they are stuck in the sand.

Satan undoubtedly strives to keep us from walking through the seasons God ordains. The deceiver of the brethren would love to use deception to cause us to see God's season as something we want to avoid. Going may look different in each season, but we must GO to the places and people God has purposed for that season.

I can imagine David as a young shepherd boy in the hills of Israel. There had to be nights when wild animals threatened the sheep, and he fought in the dark. Certainly he was scared, but God matured, prepared, and strengthened him through those times. He learned from the sheep, the hard work, the responsibility, and the threats that came his way. By the time he met the giant Goliath in 1 Samuel 17, he had learned valuable lessons in his shepherd season.

David's father, Jesse, sent him to the battle between the Philistines and Israel to take food to his older brothers and check on their welfare. David ended up before King Saul and told him that Israel did not need to fear Goliath, who had challenged Israel for forty days to send out a man to fight him in hand-to-hand combat. Remember that Goliath was nine feet and nine inches in height, and David was a small teenage boy. A grown man had no chance to fight Goliath and win, let alone a youth. David's oldest brother, Eliab, was angry at David for saying he could fight the giant and accused him of being rude and disrespectful.

David did not allow the anger of others, or the impossibilities of the season, stop him. King Saul reiterated to David that he was only a youthful boy and that Goliath was a man of war. But look how David replied to Saul in 1 Samuel 17:34–37:

"Your servant used to keep his father's sheep, and when a lion or bear came and took a lamb out of the flock, I went out after it and struck it, and delivered the lamb from its mouth; and when it arose against me, I caught it by its beard, and struck and killed it. Your servant has killed both lion and bear; and this uncircumcised Philistine will be like one of them, seeing he has defied the armies of the living God." Moreover David said, "The Lord, who delivered me from the paw of the lion and from the paw of the bear, He will deliver me from the hand of this Philistine." And Saul said to David, "Go, and the Lord be with you!"

The story continues as Saul dresses David in his own armor. But David was not comfortable in the armor, as he had not used it and was not skilled. David removed the armor, took his staff and slingshot, and chose five smooth stones from the brook and put them in his shepherd's bag. David knew he had to use the weapons that God had trained him with in the shepherding season while caring for the sheep, even if they seemed ridiculous to others.

When David approached Goliath, the giant made fun of the youth and threatened to kill him. David answered with the strength of the lessons he learned from the lions and bears in 1 Samuel 17:45:

You come to me with a sword, with a spear, and with a javelin. But I come to you in the name of the Lord of hosts, the God of the armies of Israel, whom you have defied.

From his fights with lions and bears, David learned that the battle was the Lord's. When he trusted and obeyed, God fought the battles and brought victory. With the hurling of one stone from David's sling, he killed the feared enemy of Israel. Had David not encountered the lions and bears in the previous season, he would not have been able to trust Almighty

God to face the giant and kill him with a stone. David had to be a shepherd to become a military champion and eventually become king.

We place ourselves in vulnerable positions when we despise our season and refuse to learn our lessons. If we refuse to enter a season or hold fast to the old season, we deprive ourselves of the progress God is performing in our lives.

God placed David in the fields as a shepherd of sheep to prepare him to lead his people, Israel. Moses fled Egypt and spent forty years in the backside of the desert in a season as a shepherd. There God prepared him to bring Israel out of bondage in Egypt. Daniel worked for a pagan king and remained faithful to God and the responsibilities God put in his hands.

Joseph was his father's favorite son from his old age. Yet, he was sold into slavery by his brothers, taken to Egypt, worked as a servant, was falsely accused of rape, and thrown into prison in that foreign land. He had no hope in the natural sense. However, that season was part of God's purpose to prepare him to save the world from famine and protect the lineage of Jesus Christ when he rose to second in command to Pharaoh.

Be encouraged today if you are in a Joseph season and trying to understand how to GO. Usually, we misinterpret God's purpose in these seasons, but other people can misunderstand even more. In these seasons, others tell us we have potential, need more faith, or need to talk and act differently. We are easily judged by our season. But in that season, seek the Lord and realize, like Joseph, your lonely nights in a prison cell can be preparing you for a throne.

We can easily mistake God's season as warfare. Yes, warfare

will be present in the season, but the season may be God's purpose to prepare us for the following season. First Peter 5:8 says, "Be sober, be vigilant, because your adversary the devil walks about as a roaring lion, seeking whom he may devour."

I was sad when my season was up in the prison system, and I entered employment in the drug rehab arena. It had been an outstanding season, and I loved the ladies and prison ministry. But I had to obey the Lord and move to the next season to be light in the rehab center. I had to give my time and energy to the next season.

Stephen described in Acts 7:39 how the children of Israel became dissatisfied in their season in the wilderness as Moses led them: "Whom our fathers would not obey but rejected. And in their hearts they turned back to Egypt."

As we GO daily, discouragement comes at times when we long for the days of the previous season. Like Israel when Moses was on Mount Sinai, we wonder if God will use us again as He did in the past. We notice others in a mountaintop season and wonder why our season is so difficult. Often in these seasons, people will reject us. Moses had a similar experience, but look at what Stephen said of him in Acts 7:35:

> *This Moses whom they rejected, saying, "Who made you a ruler and a judge?" is the one God sent to be a ruler and a deliverer by the hand of the Angel who appeared to him in the bush.*

Moses was rejected by the people God sent Him to lead. I can imagine some of his conversations with God:

"Why didn't you leave me on the backside of the desert?"

"Will these people ever listen to me?"

"They see me as a murderer and failure."

"They are discouraged and have lost trust in my leadership abilities."

God's continued command to Moses was to GO. Our duty is not to make one season look like another. Our responsibility is to obey God in each season. One season links to another, and each prepares us for the next. If we try to hold on to an old season or jump ahead and skip a season, we interfere with God's purpose in each season. God has no blank or purposeless days on His calendar. Ecclesiastes 3:11 explains: "He has made everything beautiful in its time."

I cannot count the times in prison ministry or working in drug rehab when my duty was to inform a woman of a death in her family. Each time I did, I more fully understood the lessons of the season when we lost my brother. I could speak from experience and share empathy with the ladies. The painful season of grief prepared me for seasons ahead that I was unaware would come.

I also taught grief and loss classes in the prisons and drug rehab. In the rehab center, counselors taught classes on eight-week cycles. The need for a grief and loss class was so needed that while I was there, the director scheduled my class nonstop. I did not enjoy the season of grief, but the lessons learned prepared me to help many women in the days ahead.

When I entered the adoption field, I was no longer the girl's clergy or counselor. I had to learn to GO and let my light shine in the darkness where my position and authority were different. I often struggled as I felt I could not do all I could as a light in the darkness. I did not see results as in past seasons, which was difficult. But the season was important in God's purpose. God forced me to learn to be light in the darkness and to GO daily as one out in the marketplace.

That season humbled me and helped me realize I am God's servant going daily to people in darkness and distress. The season looked different. The going looked different. But it was daily work and lessons I needed to learn.

When my brother was in a nursing facility for the last few months of his life, my visits with him were always interesting. I would arrive for a stopover, and Doug would say, "Let's GO visit." That meant Doug had a list of older people who needed a visit or prayer.

One day we passed an Alzheimer's patient in the hallway in front of her room door. I spoke to her and asked how she was doing. She responded that she was lost and needed to return home. I told her we knew the way and would take her. Doug and I escorted the lady around a large square of hallways and back into her room. She was delighted to be safe and back in her home. For a few minutes to an Alzheimer's patient, we were light.

After Doug's death, my grandmother fractured her back and received rehabilitation in a nursing facility. I went daily to visit her around my work schedule. Upon my arrival, we would talk. Then Grandma would hand me a piece of paper with names, room numbers, and conditions. Some were dying, some sick, some injured, and some lonely. Grandma had already told them that when her granddaughter, Londa, arrived, she would come and pray for them. God honored the willingness of Grandma to volunteer me and my willingness to obey. God saved people, encouraged the lonely, and healed some.

My dear friend and one of the best counselors I have ever met, Judy Austin, died earlier this year. Judy often made a statement that I have adopted as my own: "The older I get, the more I realize how little I know."

Judy was right. My success to GO daily is dependent on the One who called me. My strength and abilities come from Him. My task is to obey and GO in all seasons of life.

Many people believe they must reach a certain spiritual plateau before being used mightily by God. At that point, they think they will be on top of the world and have no problems. Then they will do great exploits for God's kingdom. I encourage you to avoid this mentality and realize that God does miracles when we GO daily. Yes, we must study the Word and mature. We need to fast, pray, and learn lessons as we GO, but we must start somewhere.

I used to ask my clients in drug rehab why the starting point on a racetrack was on one end of the track and not the other. My answer: Because you have to start somewhere. It is the same with us as we GO daily. We have to start obeying the gospel mandate. When we do, God will amaze us with miracles to let individuals know He is real, and He loves them.

I encourage you to start now and GO daily! The world is your platform, and those around you are your harvest field.

About the Author

LONDA DUNCAN is an ordinary woman who felt God's call to step outside the walls of the church and obey the Lord's command to GO! Obedience to God's prompting led her to women's jails and prisons, substance abuse centers, and working with women in the process of placing their children for adoption.

Londa believes the world is our platform and our ministry is those with whom we cross paths daily. Londa believes her education and ordination are tools used in the greatest endeavor on earth and that is to be a servant of our Lord and Savior Jesus Christ. She believes we must make the most of each day as we only have one life to life on this earth. Londa lives in central Florida and enjoys her family, her rescue pets, and great friendships.

You may contact Londa at LondaLDuncan@gmail.com.

CPSIA information can be obtained
at www.ICGtesting.com
Printed in the USA
BVHW051359080623
665608BV00016B/1231

9 781956 365436